W9-BSZ-809

Literate America Emerging

Literate America Emerging

Seventeen New Readers Speak Out

Edited by
Barbara Prete & Gary E. Strong

BISHOP MUELLER LIBRARY
Briar Cliff College
SIOUX CITY, IA 51104

California State Library Foundation
Sacramento
1991

LC
151
.L52
1991

© *1991 California State Library Foundation*

All Rights Reserved.
No Part of this publication may be
reprinted without permission.

ISBN: 0-929722-45-0

Credits: "Believers," "The Drum," "A Story From My Life," "Thanks for the Opportunity," "Love," "As One," "How I'm Doing in the Reading Program," "Just for Today," "Having Hope," and "Hard Knocks" previously appeared in *The Drum: Writings by Literacy Students in the Bay Area*. BALit, 1990. Distributed by the California State Library Foundation. "Inside" and "Romania" previously appeared in the *California State Library Foundation Bulletin,* Issue Number 33, October 1990. "You Stop Me From Feeling Proud" and "Heat of the Tiger" previously appeared in the *California State Library Foundation Bulletin,* Issue Number 36, July 1991. Bob's essay appeared in that same issue.

Design & Layout: Susan Acker & Mary McDermott

Photography: Gary E. Strong

25139982

Contents

Introduction

For those who read, the written word is power. For an adult who cannot read, the written word is a barrier, a symbol of a world unopened, untouchable, uninhabitable. For new readers, the discovery of words and the world they reveal marks an irreversible change in the course of their lives. This book is about that discovery. It documents the awful effects of illiteracy on individual lives and the changes that occur with the power of the written word.

Literate America Emerging is a book of hope for a nation at risk in an educational crisis. Its seventeen voices speak for the millions more adult Americans who will be crossing over the boundary from illiteracy this decade.

They provide inspiration for those who will follow. They are the front line in fulfilling the increasing need for an educated workforce. They are testimony to the new roles and opportunities available to our newly literate citizens. They are becoming active participants in our democratic institutions. It is through their stories that we can begin to comprehend how much the ability to read and write affects one's ability to participate in almost every aspect of American life. Through their stories we witness change.

The power of reading is taken for granted by the 80% of Americans who have achieved this skill in the normal way. It grants them the capacity to move at will, freely around the environment and culture. Illiterate people characteristically avoid leaving the familiar streets of their own neighborhoods.[1]

The typical adult assumed the power of the written word at a young age. It came first through messages read from family and friends, later from teachers and writers. They learn to value and treasure letters from loved ones, the written word of their professions and great literature. But the discourse of one's place in the world is more than just being able to read. It is through written words of our own creation that we are able to tell someone else what we often cannot speak aloud. We are able to ponder and carefully select the "right" words to express our meaning or plans. We can direct our message or select our audience. We can record thoughts and ideas for later. We are able to re-read what we wrote down.

This entire world of communication is cut off from one in five adult Americans because they have not learned to read. As a result, these are alienated, often disenfranchised citizens and think of themselves as outsiders looking in. They both perceive and realize fear and obstacles. This is one reason they seldom leave the safety of their own neighborhoods.

Through new readers' interpretation of the record of their lives, we can gain some insight into the plight of the person who cannot read. They put into words the shame, the struggle and agony of life without the ability to read. It is hard to admit you are illiterate to your employer, your wife, your children. In some cases we are the first to witness the new found courage it takes for them to tell their own tragic stories.

When new readers speak for themselves, they send out forceful messages of hope. They talk about "coming out of the closet," about years of commitment to learning, of growth, achievement, and empowerment. They celebrate entering mainstream American life.

Who are these people?[2] If native-born, why didn't they learn to read in the first place? What *do* they want? The men and women who share their stories here illustrate the breadth of the human side of the illiteracy problem. Gaining understanding of the depth of illiteracy's roots and wide-ranging effects on individual lives, and the dynamics of turning that around, is the aim of this book.

As expected, many of them tell of closed doors and opportunities lost, of the effects cycles of illiteracy, bequeathed from their parents, had on early experiences, how schools and learning disabilities stifled their development. Some talk about the influence of drugs and alcohol, of crimes committed, prison terms served, dependency and homelessness.

But then there are the surprises—the people who graduated from college, held positions of influence, or otherwise "made it" despite not being able to read or write. They tell another kind of illiteracy story. Theirs may be more articulate, but no less painful for them nor harmful for society.

New discoveries pop out of the pages of this book. All in all, it makes clear the fact that the shadow of illiteracy crosses over all lines: poor, middle or upper income; minority, mainstream; immigrant, native; drop-out, teacher.

As we learn more about the people in our midst who cannot read, we begin to see critical patterns in reading development. We meet seemingly normal Americans who got caught up in illiteracy's awful net. Too many identify the same vulnerable age when life changed for the worse. We feel the impact of peer pressure on their emotional well-being at these times, and stand helplessly by as reading manifests itself as a problem. We meet those with serious learning impairments and rejoice to learn they can or have gotten over them.

All describe their own version of rage for having somehow slipped through the cracks. They also blame themselves and allude to an insensitive and outmoded educational system. None forget the scars of the past. All here have found a way to use them for a better future.

Their stories come at a time when public education is under serious scrutiny across the country[3] because it no longer serves the real needs of our society or it's people. American public education has been called a 19th century institution preparing 20th century children for the 21st century. Over the next decade every aspect of it will be revolutionized. The next generation of Americans will not be illiterate.

New readers speaking out for the first time serve as potent and timely resources to this effort. By listening closely to those who have already managed to cross the line, we are learning a lot about motivation, cognitive learning, and the human spirit. Through their trials and successes, they are pointing the way to the educational system of the future. They've picked up and run with such contemporary developments as lifelong learning and computerized reinforcement programs. Their new ability to communicate through the written word has brought with it hope and achievement, growth, and the courage to speak out and be heard on a variety of issues. No longer passive, they are turning everything around, and making an impact on American life. This is the legacy they will leave to their children.

Jonathan Kozol's 1985 bestseller *Illiterate America* shocked the nation with the information that once first, "the United States ranks forty-ninth in literacy" among the nations of the world. In response, government and the private sector initiated research to determine the demographics of illiteracy and its effects on our democratic institutions and economy. Since then a number of landmark reports, from Education Secretary Bell's 1983 *A Nation At Risk: The Imperative For Educational Reform*[4] to the 1990 *Report of the Commission on the Skills of the American Workplace,* are showing the literacy crisis to be multiples greater than was ever suspected. These reports point out illiteracy's effect on each segment of society, and how it generally bodes ill for the nation's economy.

Literate America Emerging is a report on the impact of illiteracy on individual lives. Yet each of those who speak here belies the impossibility of separating illiteracy from other institutions, economic factors, and major social problems. We hope that telling these stories will encourage more research into possible connections. We also would hope publishing them can help make achieving literacy closer for the American men and women who must still find the courage to take the first step. Each of those who have decided to share their stories sought help and encouragement along the way. Now they stand ready to provide these essentials to others.

We believe the nation's thousands of volunteer and paraprofessional literacy tutors will find this book useful, as encouragement to them as well as their learners. We want its message to reach officials who must make decisions about the value of literacy programs. We nurture an abiding optimism that it will serve as a renewal to those of us who take our literacy for granted.

The oral histories speak in brave tones of the heights to which each aspires. They record significant individual achievement, as "outsiders" move into leadership roles.

In selecting the people to speak out in this book, we sought to include a variety of voices. We interviewed each new reader, recording the session on video tape in order to capture their own words. The segments published here are from the taped record of these meetings. Whenever possible, selections from the writings of each are included to further illustrate and celebrate their accomplishments. We have not edited their written words.

Whether written or spoken, their messages are moving. We were struck by their poignance and potency. We believe they are meaningful, on a personal level and to our democratic way of life.

In editing *Literate America Emerging,* we refrained from making judgements of our own. The authority comes from those who present their lives as testimony to a literate America emerging.

Our inspiration came from reading the written words of new readers. It became our deep conviction that the personal stories behind their words needed to be shared. It is here that we are allowed to witness the rewards of human effort and achievement.

Barbara Prete
Gary E. Strong

Rodica

To Keep Inside The Fire

Rodica was born on a small farm in Romania. She came to the U.S. six years ago with her parents, sisters and brothers. Only her two sisters spoke any English, learned at the university in Romania.

My first years in school were in a rural schoolhouse. I did well and was first or second in my class. Then we moved to the capital. It was a bigger school. I wasn't so confident anymore, had a hard time and felt lots of pressure.

I started writing very young. My brothers and sisters were all older, and when they went to school and left me home I got very lonely. So I went to school with them.

I always had trouble with writing though, and I think it's because I started so young and never learned to form my letters correctly. The Romanian alphabet is the same as English. I still start with the wrong letter or mix up letters. I've also always been slow in reading. Recently I found out that I may be part dyslexic.[5]

My sisters always put me down for this.
They laughed at me and wouldn't let up.

"Oh you're still reading that book" they'd say.

They made such fun of me that I didn't want to read anymore.

So I would write.

Then they'd say, "Your writing is awful; what's wrong with you?"

They are accomplished, one is an engineer, one a medical assistant. They are still harsh on me and put me down generally.

When I told my sister I had this interview, she told me

I'd make a fool of myself because I couldn't speak English. I was able to accept your invitation because I don't feel any lower than them anymore.

My sisters and I shared the same room as children. I wanted to keep a diary but couldn't because they would read it.

So that's why I started writing poetry at age ten. I wrote things the way I understood them in a language they couldn't understand. Most of them I didn't keep but I do read the little pieces of paper here and there that I've kept. I've tried to translate the ones I like, but it's impossible to translate poetry.

When I came to the United States six years ago, I still wrote in Romanian a little; but I've never shown them to anybody. I've always written for myself. I've written in English for about two years.

Our family immigrated to Chicago. I didn't know any English but had to work all day to help support my parents. My father was too old to find a job; he was 69. My mother was 62.

So I went to manicure school. Mostly, my customers taught me English then; I practiced writing by myself. Customers suggested I read more and gave me books. I started slowly and now am able to enjoy Sidney Sheldon. I'm still slow. I go back over passages and look up words.

It all changed after I went to buy a car and couldn't write out a check for the $1,000 down payment. Couldn't spell[6] one thousand. I decided to learn.

At a ladies' church luncheon, I sat next to an older lady—told her I was from Romania, and that I still have a handicap, that I couldn't write. She told me she worked with the library and gave me her phone number. She introduced me to my tutor Jeanette.

I still do manicures but just passed my real estate license exam after attending real estate school at night. Now I can write English well enough to get by but need to develop my letter formation some more.

"Believers" is the first poem I ever showed to anybody. I never thought they were special [my poems], or any good even. I'm going to start to keep my poems now.

I showed them to a musician friend, and he's become a major influence on my writing poems. His father writes poetry, and he did some also, for his music. I met him two years ago.

I make up words in my poems—"shakening," "happiless"—that say better what I try to mean. My tutor says I have to use real words or put them in quotes or italics.

Can I dream?

If I had a dream, someday I would like to publish my poems in an anthology, a collection of young American poets.

Meanwhile, I'm still in the literacy program at the library and still trying to learn how to write.[7] Spelling, grammar, punctuation, is what *write* means to me.

Romania

No positive speech, though full of desire,
no hope.
No white coats, no expiration date,
No antidote
Could terminate the curse
That lays so heavy on the shoulders
of this mother earth.

No singing birds, no quiet nights,
no moon
Is left for us to hold as dear as we should.

Why don't we sit at our tables now
And write a letter to one God.
How dear is the land, the sky, the sun.
No war, no revolution and no bomb.
Just freedom for the people,
No control.
That's what we want.
And now,
We want it all.

Believers

In between the kings and peasants,
We are the only ones
That build sweet dreams,
To let them fall
From the highest white cloud
On the shoulders of innocent people.

Every autumn eve at the dusk
We run to the end of the world
To let our souls drown
In the violet built between us and the angels.
Begging God for a new love every season,
for a new heart on every birthday,
For a new mind on every holiday

In a new world made of stone
We are the only ones that grow flowers in the
palm of our hand.
We are the angels fallen from grace,
The evils that hung the moon on the
other side of the night.
The people that cheat on their left hand.

The last to be worth anything
the first to be saved.

Inside

Some countries make their border pretty hard
And decorate them with ruffles of barbed wire
To keep outside the dreams,
To keep inside the fire.

Some countries teach their children
That God does not exist.

But the children have seen God
Closer to their homes
Than food on their plates.

For them, religion is their refuge
and the law of the land is the beast.

Young Doves

We haven't learned to fly yet
We are still connected to this earth.
Our souls are earthbound,
We collect in our hearts
Every place that has touched us,
And the feel of this hill
That we climb everyday.

Our legs are probably tired
Sometimes skipping,
Sometimes limping,
Sometimes anxious
To reach the top.
Sometimes anxious
To fly.

But we haven't learned to fly yet,
We are still forming –
Learning – Molding.
The stars haven't accepted us yet
We are still earth people.

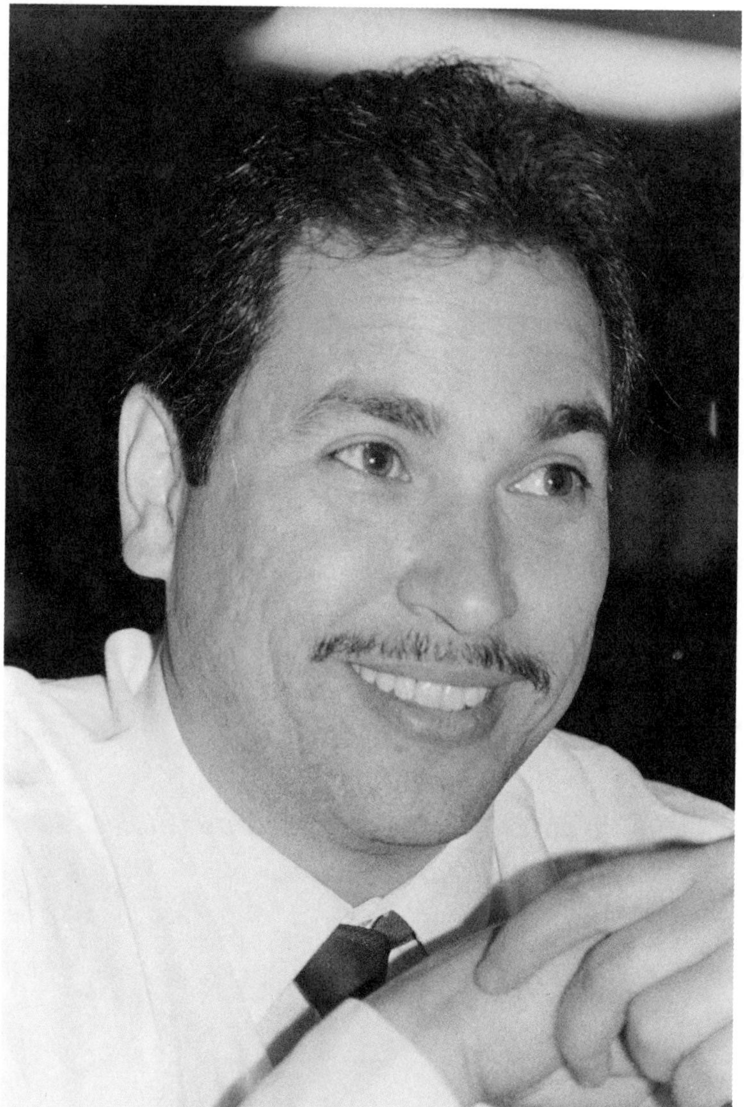

Enrique

Don't Hold Us Back

Enrique has done a lot to help literacy programs: he is a founder and board member of the San Francisco Bay Area New Readers' Council; served on a National Issues Forum at the White House; and represents new readers on the Workforce Literacy Task Force of the California State Senate. United Airlines, his employer, honored him for community involvement. He was a delegate from California to the White House Conference on Libraries and Information Sciences in 1991.

In elementary school I was in about the 5th grade, and they put us into a speed reading class. It was held in the auditorium. There were 35 kids and an elderly woman teacher, and she didn't really have much control. We played around like it was recess, and I guess it didn't help us but really hurt us. We all had problems later. Thirty-five good readers turned out to be 35 kids with reading problems.

In junior high school all the slower readers were put together. I got onto the track team. The coach gave me a tutor who didn't like to stay after school, so he did my work for me.

In the 9th grade I hurt my leg so no more track. I went to school, signed in but didn't stay, instead I hung out. I had given up.

I kept getting promoted though, with A's, B's, and D's until 12th grade. They didn't graduate me because I was short some credits. When I left, they had me down as an 11th grade drop out.

I signed up for college and went for one semester, studied architecture and did a lot of good drawings, but couldn't read even my own notes. I took a reading class there. The teacher couldn't speak English very well, and I couldn't understand him. So I dropped out of college.

I got a job in a janitorial supply house, starting in sales. The job required a lot of reading and writing to learn the chemical formulas. What I would do was go to the warehouse and ask the gentleman there to explain them to me. That way I learned all the chemicals, and what they did.

A lot of other people there couldn't read. What they did was develop their own dictionary in their minds.

I got married and had a little boy. My wife was the only one working then, and we couldn't just live on her income. She helped me fill out the job applications. I never got the jobs. My friends couldn't help me because they all had good jobs, like machinists, that required reading.

Then I found out about the reading program. About that time I got an entry level job at the airport handling cargo. I advanced to supervisor in a couple of weeks.

I could see his eyes water, and I'd hurt inside . . .

After four months they offered me a job as manager. I stalled on taking it because I couldn't read and write, and the job required it. They didn't know this about me. I was ready to quit.

I went away for a few days then came back and told them the truth about my problem. I said I couldn't read but was in a reading program. They said "That's okay, you're the man for the job."[8]

After that I moved on to a better paying job at United Airlines where I've been for one and a half years now. They knew about my reading and writing problems when I got hired. They—both the company and my fellow workers—support me. I haven't missed a day since I was hired.

Most people who can't read or write get laughed at, and

I was used to it. Once there was a note pinned up where I punch in "Go on back to school."

At United there were never any pinned up or printed messages on the walls. And everybody at UA reads. You can see people reading the *Times* and other newspapers during lunch. We do the crosswords. The newspaper is a real hot item.

When I first got into the reading program, my son was about three years old.[9] I used to push him away when he asked me to read to him. I could see his eyes water, and I'd hurt inside because that's not what a father is all about. But I wouldn't show it.

Now I read books with him, and we have lots of fun. My two and a half-year old daughter gets so jealous of my reading to my son that she climbs up onto my lap with her book and shoves him off.

In the beginning of 1989 I was asked to testify before the State Small Business Commission.[10] My testimony was about reading and writing and the workplace and how the literacy program helped me.

I told them how I passed the GED and got my high school diploma, passed my drivers test without anyone taking it for me, how I can do my checking account, and go shopping. Now I can read labels, not just look at the pictures on labels, and save money.

Then I was asked to be on the committee[11] to represent literacy students. The other people on the committee are officials. I liked the part about having a student involved. It should be a joint thing with input from the students. Sometimes the state has the right ideas and the right intentions, but we should be able to help, to tell what the needs are and how the program can be improved.

I wrote a letter to all the programs in the state, and they distributed it to all the students. When I got their feedback I presented it to the committee. We all want to continue something that's working.

Obviously its working because students are succeeding in their lives. I've run into lots of students who've moved up in life because life has changed. My life has changed. I've gone from bad to being more confident in myself, feeling more comfortable and positive in the things I'm doing. I've got a good job;[12] my kids are happy; I'm happy.

Don't hold us back.

In the future I want to do more[13] for students. I want to try to bridge the communication gap between employers and employees. I want to let businesses know about people like me, who may have turned down jobs they could do with confidence.

But like me, they had a reading problem. Not learning how to read and write was something that just happened to some people, a mistake. But don't hold us back. We may become the perfect employee.

I just spoke at my union meeting of 150 shop stewards. I asked if any of them knew of anybody who couldn't read. Fifteen hands went up. It's a macho thing for men to admit. I think it's easier for a woman, she can get away with asking for help.

When people ask if I feel bad about not knowing how to read and write, I say no, I'm doing something about it. When you've been to school and got left behind, a one-on-one learning situation with a tutor helps in so many ways.

I get excited when I learn something new.

There are so many people out there who need this kind of help. I've been a welder for ten years, but I can't pass the state test. I'm a pipe fitter but could never pass the state test. So I've turned down these jobs. How many more people are there like this? If only they heard more about the literacy program.

The state should know that it's got to invest in advertising for these programs.[14] Most of the people on the streets have radios, advertise on the kids' stations. If you push kids to say no to drugs, push them to say yes to reading. Let them get the message on their rock shows.

It's hard to get into it. The first step is hard. Once you start, it's a thrill—a whole new world.

Now I get excited when I learn something new. I can speak up and speak my mind and know what I'm talking about. I can say, "I don't think so."

When people hand out flyers I can read them, instead of folding it up and making a plane out of it. I can vote.

It's great. It's changed my life.

> *My desire to improve my reading skills and writing skills were strong. I needed to do so in order to obtain my GED. I also wanted to pursue a better paying job. In addition, I felt a need for my self-improvement and I wanted to be able to read to my son.*
>
> *...Many non readers are hesitant to seek help because they are afraid and often are embarrassed, also....*
>
> *Since I began working with a personal tutor, there have been many positive changes in my life. I am now able to fill out a job application, have advanced in my job, and now I am a volunteer for the San Mateo Search and Rescue Team. I can also now sit down with my son and read to him.*

Excerpt from Enrique's testimony before a Joint Committee Hearing on "Workforce Literacy: Growing Disparity Between Worker Skills and Employer Needs" of the California Legislature.

Daleanna

I'm Trying . . .

Tall, beautiful, her smile shows the radiance within. Dressed in a ginger-colored jacket and matching tam in her orange blond hair, she's timid and often looks close to tears when not smiling.

Her mother was a schizophrenic with 28 faces, her dad believed incest was alright in the eyes of God.

Daleanna, named for her parents, Dale and Anna, was the oldest of eight children. She has been in more foster homes than she can remember, and one year she was in seven schools.

She left school in the ninth grade to become a mother with her first child. She is now a 35 year old grandmother and plans to get her associate of arts degree. She is passionately interested in psychology and in writing as well as in music.

I'm a mother of five children, my oldest is eighteen and a mother herself. My youngest one is two.

I have always had to send my children out to get me things because I can't–wouldn't know how to do it. How do I make a shopping list? I cannot make a shopping list. I cannot get a job as being a waitress because I can't put things down on paper.

I've wanted to be able to spell and write and make sentences. I had been in school but kept getting turned back because I couldn't read and write.

One class I was even asked to leave. I never had a proper education. We just had a bad family life–a dis–functional family.

I always liked school, but I've had my problems with it. I have ob–stacles that get in the way, but now I know that if I keep trying, I'm going to get it. And that's all right.

This is hard to say, if ever you want to do something, you do it over and over and over again, until you know it. That's how I figured I'd get to read and write.

If I need a job, and they need these skills, then I'll learn to read what they want me to read[15] and I'll learn to write what I need to write, and I'm trying and trying.

I'm doing this on my own. No support comes from anyone close to me. I have no husband and my oldest daughter used to ridicule me.

I used to get upset when she would laugh at me and say "You're stupid. I'm smarter than you are, and I can do this and that and you can't."

All I can say in response is "I'm trying."

Support for what I'm doing comes from people in the literacy programs and support groups. I go[16] to the learning center at the community college, and they help me a lot.

It's a lot of work, but it's EXCITING!

To be able to be able to put things down, to show that you can express yourself clearly, and it doesn't have to be with your mouth. That's really exciting.

And to know that you can make a list, start putting things down that other people will understand, that they aren't just marks you made and only you know what they mean. That's exciting!

Often I wish I could get hit on the head with something and learn it all overnight. There have been times at the learning center when I get depressed.

I feel that my tutors are tired of trying with me, that they get sick and tired of the same routine over and over and that nobody really wants to help me anymore. It's like I grab them and want to monopolize them with my questions and suck it all up.

There have been quite a few times I've wanted to cry [at this Daleanna is close to tears] because I want it so much. I feel like they're tired of trying, but I'm not tired of trying.

There's been a big change in my ability to learn lately. I can see it most with my spelling. It used to take me *soo* long to read a word, now it's coming fast, almost too fast to believe.

. . . but I'm not tired of trying.

It's like I've finally crossed over something and learned to learn. It feels good. I was on the other side *soo* long. I've learned to do sentences and stuff; that is really something for me.

When I taught my oldest child the ABC's, is when I learned my ABC's. She's the one who used to laugh at me for being stupid. But now she is starting to respect me; she doesn't complain the way she used to; seems to watch what she says to me now; our relationship is getting stronger.

I think I'm giving my children an incentive to read and to keep trying even when it's hard. Now I read to them and they want to read back to me. They like me to read real hard stuff. I think that's great.

Before, I wouldn't read to them at all because I had trouble. There are still a lot of stories I can't read to them.

Someone gave me a copy of *Grimm's Fairy Tales.* It's hard.[17] We read to each other two or three times a week. The other times we do other things, like get up and sing and dance.

We try to have fun.

But my kids will be literate.

Heat of the tiger

Heat of the tiger is upon me.
I asked him, "Why?"
I have something for you
since you caught my eye.
It's something
I no longer want.
As I reply,

"No, it's not my responsibility,
so find a fool,
just let it not be me.
I have my own, you see, for
I also long to be free."

Daleanna read her poems on video camera after the interview. When she read, her voice changed, her slight speech impediment was gone and she spoke clearly, with passion and power. After finishing "The Heat of the Tiger" she explained that the poem is about someone trying to make you responsible for them; you say no, I won't be responsible for you.

Why must I pay
for my brothers and sister
and ancestor's past life?
I was not there,
that was not me
though I look like them,
I sound like them,
but I'm not them.
I have what they don't.
It's love.
For love is not sex,
and it isn't color,
race or creed.
It's a freedom to be
just you and me.
Love gives no pain, or tears,
nor does it want you to fear.
Love gives joy and happiness in what you see,
hear, feel.
It makes laughter, smiles, and
(a) feeling of cheer.
Love is not only for you and me to feel but for all.

The fight is going
we're not knowing
for it's not showing
to you and me.
They are crowding around
We don't hear a sound
for we are dozing,
can't you see?
Then we are fleeting reality
to be pleased
with you and me.
A freedom disguised
for we do survive
the hard reality.

You stop me from feeling
proud, of what I am, though
pain got me to this place?
Pain you give stops me from
trying to heal my wounds,
now that I can find
them. Why must
you destroy my cure: For my
pain is from the wounds.
I feel proud of the discovery
and I am working
toward the cure. I'm two-thirds there.

Daleanna wrote this poem for the library literacy staff for Christmas:

Not only is knowledge golden
as you're the keeper of the books
that set the people free.
Just like me.
Your gentle hand has taught me
your heart is golden
for you gave to me and my family
a Christmas more internal
the joy
with best memories
is only a touch
of what you have done for me.

Daleanna has had a series of misfortunes since we interviewed her which have interrupted her progress. She had to testify as a witness in a murder trial. At the beginning of the year Daleanna was brutally beaten, hospitalized and her two small sons kidnapped. She is recovering once again and sent word that she is looking forward to having her poems published in this book.

HELLO
my name is

Efrain

From The Heart

Efrain was born in New York. He is married and the father of two sons aged seven and nine. He's played the conga drums for twenty years. This is his first poem, written in 1990:

The Drum

One day I touched the sound
And it touched me. I know
Not why. Sound of times
Long ago come to me now.
The wood and skin become
The rhythm and the rhythm is life.

I can express myself in music easily but was surprised that this poem brought any recognition. It came from inside my heart. Once I get to a good level of reading, I'm going to go back to college and try to take the physics and science courses I've wanted to take all my life because I'm also a bit of an inventor.

And I've been a graphic artist for years as a sideline, just did a logo for a store; I'd love to do it as a business. I used to do great logos, but with misspelled words. But now that I can read and spell, everything's changed.

I don't feel ignorant or retarded anymore.

I still read at a very elementary level, but know what I can do and have the incentive to keep going. This is the kickoff for me.

It was pretty rough going as a child. Battered at home then battered in school. There were family problems, my parents were going through a divorce, there wasn't enough time for me. Just enough time to feed me and try to get through life.

I remember reading a little in the first grade and a public school teacher beating my knuckles with a ruler because I couldn't read in the second grade.

It was rough, I didn't want to go to school, and I didn't want to go home and get beaten again there. I think I lost most of the first and second grades.

I guess my parents thought I was a problem because they tried to put the fear of God into me. Then they realized they should get me out of New York City because it was a bad scene for a little kid.

When I moved to L.A., they scared me bad enough to make me go to school. The schools there weren't very good and turned me off.[18] There was overcrowding, and I don't remember really learning anything—unless I ran into a teacher that I was really interested in.

Art was one of the fields I could always relate to because I didn't have to read, just use my hands and my imagination. As I got into high school, I was terribly interested in science, especially physics, and had a good teacher. But as the class got harder, the academic parts were too difficult for me to understand in the books. Reading was really the only problem. In the seventh or eighth grade a teacher gave me a verbal test.

She said, "I know there's no problem, that you understand what's going on, but you're not doing your homework, you're not doing the paperwork."

Finally I confessed it to her and told her I couldn't read. She let me pass with a verbal test.

I knew I had a serious problem, but it was difficult to get help then. My parents were busy working, trying to get by financially and couldn't help me.

They knew about it but—they didn't respond—didn't respond to it. What I mean is they had no one there making me read. There was no one I could turn to.

Then I was put into a reading class, but it was just so short and not extensive enough, so I didn't learn as much as I wanted to.

I got into a high school called Woodrow Wilson. It was so crowded with children that they had 65 kids in one class, and this is a 35-capacity room. Then they cut the school day in half. By the time you sat down in a classroom, the bell rang to change classes.

I'm tired of hiding this, lying to myself, tired of it.

It got more and more difficult not reading, and more and more embarrassing. It got to a point where I didn't tell anybody, but instead pretended like I knew how to read. Just basically held it away from everybody—didn't tell anyone.

Then once I got out of school, I worked with my father doing chores, helping him in his air conditioning business. I could understand anything that was explained to me and did all sorts of complicated things,[19] like I even worked in a film lab.

I couldn't read words but referred to a catalog like a recipe book. As long as I could see the words, I could relate to the mechanicals.

So I was faking my way. I had a good paying job and managed a lot of the time—no, most of my life—to fake my way through. When I really ran into a problem, I'd call someone to help me spell or something.

For applications I'd carry a lot of information with me in my wallet and just write all the stuff down.

Thank God I met my wife. She's been my super-helper.

When I first met her I opened myself up and said "Look, I've got a very bad problem; I do not know how to read."

She was behind me 100% all of the time. I'd call her for help and bring applications to her to fill out. I found all kinds of devious little things to say to people because I couldn't read, like "I have to go take care of something." when I had to take an application form to my wife.

What took me out of that finally was when I was with two women friends and they asked me to read a poem or a joke or something in a newspaper. By this time I'm 34 years old, and I just realized I'm tired of this.

And I opened up the page, and I just said "You know, I don't even know how to read this."

It was *so* embarrassing for me, but I just got fed up with it. I said to them and to me "I'm tired of hiding this, lying to myself, tired of it."

My friend apologized, and said she didn't mean to embarrass me. But I was deeply embarrassed. I told her my situation, that it was very painful for me.

This bothered me severely, to the point that I was deeply upset and went through a lot of anxiety. I did a lot of spiritual praying and what have you, trying to get some help. Then I just made up my mind that I was going to go down and talk to someone at the library.

I went to the library in my neighborhood. There was this grumpy old guy I knew there behind the desk. He just turned me off. I just wasn't going to tell this guy I don't know how to read.[20]

So I went to the Main Library. There was a lady there, and she was so supportive. She said "No problem, we'll see what we can do."

And she had me read this very elementary little column. It was a story about a man from Japan or China, who had to leave his family. I read through this story, stumbled over a couple of little words—I was reading at a first grade level or something like that.

She said "It's obvious you understand what you're talking about." You read between the lines is what she meant.

She was still supportive and told me, "We are going to find you a teacher you can be compatible with," and if I didn't like the teacher I could let them know; and they would find me someone else.[21]

About a week later they called me up, and they said they had a teacher for me. Then I began to sweat, the palms. I was a total nervous wreck. It turned out so was she. We both finally calmed down and got to know each other.

I told her how frustrated I feel. How can I help my kids? The American language is so hard. I've been looking at spanish words and can spell them right out because they spell the way they sound. But I've come out of my shell, and wish I had earlier.

This is the kick-off and everyone is rooting for me.

Both Efrain and his tutor are artists and enjoy working together in a flexible, tailor-made program that includes finding solutions to the problems that interrupt Efrain's learning.

Excerpt from Efrain's Christmas letter (1990) to Second Start:

> *You have helped me to realize that being able to read is like having a warm blanket. If you learn and enrich yourself it is in turn a shelter and a way of expression. Without that blanket, that knowledge, you are at risk. You are, in a sense, naked and vulnerable.*

Efrain added the following postscript:

> *By the way, my son Jeremy, wrote a small piece [that was printed] in the paper. I had to send you a copy. I'm so proud that my sons have a liking for writing. And I'm happy that they'll never have to face the misfortune that I have had to deal with in the past. I'm also glad that they're aware of the world around them.*

Ginger

There's A Lot of Me That Needs To Be Drug Up and Written About

Idella (Ginger), an adult learner since 1988, is interested in writing and has recently begun to work on an autobiography. A short excerpt from it appears at the end of this story. After she talks of her purpose for writing it and what she hopes it will achieve.

I'm from Cleveland, Ohio.

My oldest daughter is a principal of a school. I put her through college.

I went back to school the first time to help my children with their schoolwork, to read to them, to explain things to them. When my children went to school, I went to school.

They read to me then and helped me with my homework.

Then I started working as a receptionist at a doctor's office. After work I was too tired to go to school too. In 1975 they put me on disability, and I stopped working.

My kids encouraged me to go back to school. Two years ago, I did.

As you get older, if you don't keep it up, you're going to forget it. I had forgotten a lot and went back because I couldn't read the way I wanted to. Worse, I could not pronounce.

I got into the computer program[22] and just wanted to stay there because I could teach myself with it. It taught me how to break up words, pronounce and spell them, and just read more. I relaxed with that computer. I had something to encourage myself.

First there were the vocabularies. Then it taught how to make sentences—I really fell in love with that, and third, it taught writing.

Now I'm in vocabularies again because you can never learn enough of this, especially if you want to write—There's lots more in me needs to be drug up and written about. I also enjoy reading books along with the computer tapes. It helps me a lot because then I read the book without the tape and know the words.

I have everything, but I still don't have what's important.

I'm into using good English and pronouncing long words. I have a special tablet of these big words which I write down from the computer lessons and take home. Then, in steps, I practice.

I learn to spell them, to use them, and rehearse them in sentences. Sometimes I surprise myself when I see I've used a word right. Then I know it; then I know that word.

I write because I want to help somebody. I will write an autobiography, and it will help children think. The first thing they read in it won't sound right to them because it will say, "I have everything, but I still don't have what's important."

Children nowadays push their parents to get them material things, and the parents do it.[23] My book will help them realize that this isn't enough; it will make them think.

I don't know how I'm going to say this, but it will come to me.

I was born in 1927 at Pertshire, Bolivar County, Mississippi. Things are different now from when I was a child. This is a story I would like to tell about when we children (seven girls and one boy) were growing up.

My mother and dad were our doctors. How were they our doctors? They had to make our own medicine. How did they do that? They went to trees like gum trees, peach trees, and mint bushes. Let me tell you about the gum tree medicine. When we children got sick with a stomach upset, my mother made tea out of gum tree leaves, and she took the leaves and wrapped our bodies in them for about two hours. After my mother removed those leaves the body was well . . . many children died from whooping cough but my mother and dad made medicine for that cough; they called it cow hoof tea . . . they put cow hoofs in the stove and baked them until they were crisp like potato chips, put them in a tea kettle of water and boiled them for about ten minutes. The tea was bitter, but it did stop the whooping cough.

from Ginger's autobiography

Lloyd

Thanks for the Opportunity

Lloyd is a longshoreman who rose to secretary/treasurer of his union and Grand Knight of the Knights of Columbus without reading. We interviewed him the day his company honored him for twenty-five years of service. He's but a few months away from realizing his career-long dream to manage his own company garage, a very high level, respected job.

I'm excited about reading. It's taken a lot more than I thought, but is well worth it. I came from a one-room school in Bull Canyon, Colorado, a uranium mining and pinto bean farming camp town of 60–70 people.

Everyone lived in wood framed canvas tents or trailers spread out over the area, parked wherever the mining was going on. My father and another man mined one particular claim.

School was more a baby sitting service to mind the kids while the parents worked mines than school. It provided neither a real school experience nor a formal education.

Then we moved to Natarita, Colorado, a bigger mining town and a more formal educational situation. By age eleven or twelve, we moved again, to Long Beach, California.

I was already behind in school and had developed an excellent ability for gab to hide this from my friends. I could talk a blue streak.

Sports also kept me going for awhile in high school. I love sports and played baseball and basketball for three years.

Then I got hurt and couldn't play sports, so resigned from school for a while in the 11th grade. I did go back and graduate, but not with high honors. After graduating, I went to two years of college.

Because I couldn't read, I always sought out OJT (on-the-job-training)—in the army, in jobs, etc., because it trained me in all I needed to know to work.

It just took me longer than probably a lot of other people to accomplish the goals I set. I worked in security in the service, then got a part-time job working on the docks.

I knew my trade well, just had to bluff my way through the reading

I worked hard and constantly pestered the shop manager for a full-time job. Finally he hired me as a painter. After a while I learned the trade of a journeyman mechanic and worked side-by-side for years and years with other journeymen.

When my boss felt I knew enough, he promoted me to a journeyman too. I continued learning and worked my way up to being a foreman, and on from that up to being a supervisor.

I never was involved in anything that required reading or writing until I became a supervisor. I thought I knew the job well; it would be in large part leading people.

But suddenly everything was different and the door kinda shut there for a moment—there were manuals and reports to be read and written. That's when I took the necessary steps to do it.

To learn to read.

While I was learning, I guess I was fortunate because I got my boss, whom I'd been working for for 16 years by then, to help carry me through the toughest reading parts of the job.

Most of the correspondence got done by the manager. Increasingly though, the supervisor had to write letters too.

I got a lot of help from my family, mostly from my

sons. I knew my trade well, just had to bluff my way through the reading until I could do it..

I finally admitted my problem to my boss after joining the literacy program. He wasn't shocked.

He said, "Lloyd, you didn't fool me. Your abilities were fine enough and you did your job."

There was no scolding. But I've always felt he carried me along.

I'd seen ads for the literacy program and wanted to get involved in it so badly. I went down for an interview then met Donna, the director.

It had never occurred to me that the letters had sounds. To me the letters were simply A,B,C,D, ...

She gave me some comprehension tests[24] and asked me some questions. I can't say there weren't any words I knew, but they were just a few, and I skipped over the rest.

The thing that stands out in my mind the most is when Donna asked me to sound out the alphabet. It had never occurred to me that the letters had sounds. To me the letters were simply A,B,C,D,....

I thought I already knew my problem, but when she said the letters each have sounds, I became aware of the true extent of it. I could think and tell you everything, but when it came down to putting it down on paper, I just couldn't do it.

I couldn't spell; I couldn't get my thoughts together. I didn't have enough confidence. It got to be a thing with me. That's what my tutor Donna's working with me now on, building confidence.

I've been with Donna for two years now. We've made good progress, and she's encouraged me all along. I've found out that I could read.

Once reading, I sent for every magazine and publication. I read them all because it was a new world. There's not too much I can't read now, so we're working on writing sentences.

Donna makes me practice organizing my thoughts by writing on my computer. She's got me where I start by writing anything down, then putting things in order. I realize that writing is the key to my future. If she didn't make me do it, I'd do it on my own because I want it so badly.

I sent for every magazine . . . I read them all because it was a new world.

I have the drive and always had a good attitude. When I'd fall, I get up, with a smile. As a matter of fact, I work as much as possible with people on attitudes. I think attitude is the key to everything.

Donna taught me that if you don't read, it's because you don't want to read—you just don't do it. Before, if there was something to read, I could always postpone it.

I have the feeling that if I had the ability to read and write years ago, life would have changed for me. I've always enjoyed working but got held up in the maintenance department.

I couldn't take the English language and reading tests required to get into another department, so I shied away and stayed where I was. For years I wanted to get into operations but wouldn't even dream of trying to move there.

I'm still in maintenance.

Today, I got my 25-year plaque. Now I wish to stay in maintenance, but as a garage manager. It's a highly respected position. I've already been offered this position twice in the last six months, in Long Beach and Houston, but turned them both down.

I wasn't ready to deal with the reading requirements yet. I still had no confidence in myself. It would have humiliated me if they had asked me to write, and I couldn't. I didn't want to embarrass anybody else either.

The literacy program is important. Lacking the tools to read really crushes one's confidence. I know about tools as a mechanic, where I learned to use them. With reading, I had the tools but never learned to use them.

Lacking the tools to read really crushes one's confidence.

Illiteracy can happen to anybody—they just don't learn to use the tools![25] I believe that only once you learn to read can you begin to learn to help yourself.

Once you have the ability to understand what's going on, when before in a lot of cases you didn't, I don't see how you can be stopped.

I'm getting my company involved. It's news to them so I'm introducing it slowly.

Another man, an excellent journeyman mechanic, started in the literacy program last week. The company is beginning to understand the importance of literacy training. They are contributing to the program now.

My kids used to sit with me and help me through the lessons. Now they feel that some of their brains are rubbing off on me. And my brother just started in a Southern California literacy program.[26]

I want to go back as a tutor, to give back something. I've already spoken on behalf of the literacy program. I spoke before the Alameda County Council on the night they were voting on the literacy program budget.

If I have anything to say, it's about the importance of the literacy program to people who have been ashamed and embarrassed most of their lives. It gives them an opportunity to step forward and to walk tall. It lets them gain the tools necessary to do the job.

Thanks for the Opportunity

When I sat down with someone who cared that I learned and guided me through my rough times, things started falling into place. First I sounded the letters...not just read them but sounded them out, vowels then consonants. Then I started to read and before I knew it, I was reading newspapers and short stories. After that I started to write, just as I am doing now. Believe me it's not the greatest, but for someone who couldn't write a sentence, I feel great. I know that as the weeks and months pass by, with good hard work, I will improve.

Thanks must be given to all involved, the Literacy Program Director, her staff, my loving family, and most of all my tutor who always gave me a vote of confidence and was there through all of the trying times.

There were many days and nights of mispronounced and misspelled words and, of course, my favorite quotes like, "That's right." "Good!!" "Great!!" and "Take your time."[27]

Thanks, everyone. Thanks for giving me an opportunity in bettering my education and gaining the confidence that is necessary to succeed.

My Son Andrew

Andrew is my older son. He is 23 years old, has blonde hair, blue eyes, tan complexion with a muscular build. As a graduate of Cal-Berkeley, Andrew has received a wide variety of honors. He was on the Dean's List, an honor student, Phi Beta Kappa, and was given an application to be a Rhodes scholar at Oxford. Along with that, Andrew received the Dean's Scholarship for four full years while attending Cal.

Andrew early in life set his goals for his future and I must say he has completed them all. I am one very proud father.

My Son Mike

Michael is my younger son. He is a dark haired blonde, blue eyed, tall and a well built 16 year old. He is now in the tenth grade at Alameda High School where he is very active in leadership programs.

I am a very fortunate father to have a son like Mike. Over the years he has become not only a fine son, but a good and close friend. Mike seems to always be there with a good sense of humor and a loving attitude.

Sherries

And This Was All Over Reading

Sherries has "gone public," sharing her story and enthusiasm at community group meetings and tutor training workshops. She now teaches workshops on self-esteem building and communication between student and tutor. Her desire for a student support group and her initiative are responsible for READ (Read Everyone and Discover).

Since our interview with her she successfully passed the state board examination to become a Certified Nurse's Assistant and was a delegate to the White House Conference on Libraries and Information Services in 1991.

Short, round, fashionably dressed in a white dress with a black trim, she talks slowly and thoughtfully.

I don't know why I don't know how to read. I was never involved in school as a child. I went through elementary, junior high, and high school.

In the 2nd grade I had a teacher, Mrs. Clay, who embarrassed me. She announced to the whole class that I was the only one who didn't pass a test.

I became quiet in class so no one would bother me. I became quiet to myself as well as the years went on. I stayed in the back of the classroom where no one worried about me. I learned at a young age that the quieter I am, the less people bother with me.

When I got into the 4th grade a very nice teacher tried to help me. She saw I couldn't read and taught me a bit. But then they cut that program out. So in the 5th and 6th grades it was back to the same old thing again.

By junior high I became a pro at faking reading and not having to do it. I forgot my glasses, got laryngitis. I kept it from my mother and brother too. And by the time I was in junior high school I was an angry young lady.

All my friends were smart "A" students. Sometimes they did my homework. I never read a newspaper or picked up a book.

My mother didn't know about the reading; she only knew she had a troubled teenager out of control. She thought she had a kid who liked to go to school to harass the teachers and get in trouble for no reason at all.

She had a couple of reading kids, I just wasn't one of them. I was a great disappointment to her so I lashed out. I blamed my mother for my problem, made it her fault. I was just a mean child, and frustrated.

. . . my life just kept getting smaller and smaller.

When I left home, I was pregnant and figured I'd leave all the hurt and pain behind. Everything would be wonderful. But it didn't happen that way. After I had my son, my life just kept getting smaller and smaller. How would I read to my son, teach him?

I was on welfare,[28] and I had to fill out a questionnaire, but I couldn't read it. My cousin was with me at the time so she read it to me. At the end there was this question "Do you need help?"

I told her to check "yes" to see what they would do for me. Then this social worker came to our house, and she turned me onto a psychiatrist who turned me on to my first tutor. My son was 2 then.[29]

Mrs. Campbell. She came like a survival kit. She helped me get my driver's license. She came to my house twice a week. We started with the very basic book one and went to book six.

One day a cousin visited during a tutoring lesson and overheard. She told me later, "Boy are you stupid, you can't even read."

That set me back maybe a month. I just told the tutor I couldn't go on with this anymore.

Mrs. Campbell kept calling and asking what happened. We finally got back in the track again. It set me back a lot.

I always bought lots of books for my son; you'd think I was a scholar. He liked this book *Green Eggs and Ham*, so I memorized it so I could read it to him. I started developing a very good memory.

From where I am right now I remember myself as a gloomy-type person when I was a young mother. There was a cloud over me. People didn't like me when they first met me.

I wasn't mean. It was that I had this small world,[30] and I couldn't let too many people invade it. People in your life, they probe, and I didn't want anyone to know my secret. I was the kind of person that, if I met her—me, then—I wouldn't like her. I was a very moody woman. I never smiled. My house was immaculate.

I married when my son was five. I figured, "This man loves me. It'll make my life just splendid."

We had a very bad divorce. I only had two friends that stuck by me. I would ask someone to do something for me once. If they didn't do it, so be it. I'd never ask again.

When my son was 12 or 13, we moved to New Mexico, and that's how everything started to turn around for me. Everything changed. I had a job I didn't like. I knew that if I didn't do something about it that this was it for me.

I thought about committing suicide. All this was over reading. One day I got up and decided I was going to school.

I thought about committing suicide.
All this was over reading.

I always felt that if I stopped growing that I might as well just die. And this was all over reading. That's been the chain around my neck, that's my dungeon.

Even now, if I allow myself, it'll come back and tap me on the shoulder and say, "You're not smart." "You're fooling yourself." I never forget.

I upped and went to a community college. They had a study room where there were materials so you taught yourself how to read. You could check out books there. Student volunteers would help you if you found something too hard.

Zeke saw me there again and again and asked me if I wanted a tutor. I said, "Yes."

My first tutor, Marge, cared about me and my family. She went from being my tutor to my friend to my best friend.

I have so much more to do,
so many more miles to travel.

Sometimes Marge and I would sit down for three hours at a time. Other times I'd call her up in the middle of the night and say, "I can't figure out this word. What is this word?"

This lady helped open doors that I didn't even know existed. The world started to brighten up. I don't know why, but I felt like I was really accomplishing something.

I'd had other tutors. I even had private tutors for two years. But this time I was ready. I didn't care anymore if anyone came in and saw me. That wasn't my problem anymore.

If you didn't like me because I couldn't read, that was not my concern. My concern was learning to read now. I channeled all those angers and things into this. At the same time Marge was my tutor I was in vocational rehabilitation and with a psychiatrist named Rusty.

We dealt with a lot of shit that was hanging on my head. These were issues I had never talked about or told my mother or anybody. He was the first man I ever got into it with, and it helped me.

I have so much more to do, so many more miles to travel. I can tell you for sure nothing's going to stop me now. I may feel low or down, I might even lose my self esteem one more time, but I'll get up and dust myself off.

Someday I want to sit down and read myself a novel. I want to read about Hawaii and reach out and touch it if I can't go there. I want to read myself to sleep.

I want to keep a journal and write down my intimate thoughts. Just to read a book, that in itself would be so wonderful to me. It's not so far off. I have already read *Jonathan Livingston Seagull.*

Loneliness

I have an intimate friend
He is called loneliness
He caresses me like a
Deep, dark sea.
It's like darkness
That never has light
It's like cold
That never felt warmth
It's like a motherless child.
If by chance I meet someone special
He retreats like the low tide
and he's very confident knowing
He will be back.
I'm left with a cold chill
The only thing that can
Defeat him is the true love of myself.

Love

Love is your greatest friend
or your worst enemy.
When you have it life is beautiful
When it's gone life is cold and dreary.
You have a pain that you thought you would have to be physically hurt to feel.
Life is not the same, what used to be beautiful is now distorted.
What used to be whole is now crumbled.
Where there used to be trust, now
there is nothing. I got all this from love.
The sad thing is what shall I do if love comes again? I lost so very much the first time...
From the eyes of a broken heart.

BOB

Crazy Bobby

Bob entered the library literacy program Project Second Chance in 1985. He was a recovering alcoholic and drug addict who attended AA meetings at least twice a week.

He's become a vocal spokesperson for literacy, interacting with learners of many ethnic backgrounds. He spends a great deal of time and energy promoting literacy and encouraging adult learners to work together.

Today Bob provides in-home care for seniors. He continues to improve his reading and writing skills on his own. He still writes for his own pleasure.

One of my parents was a dropout from the 6th or 7th grade, one graduated from high school. There were three of us children. Mother worked at night.

While she worked, us children had to ask dad for help with schoolwork. He couldn't help. I don't know how my siblings managed, but I didn't.

Being that I was a slow learner, and without the help I needed at home, I fell behind. But I didn't let anyone know I was falling behind.

I had to find a shield, a cover, to protect myself from others finding out that I was behind. I found that being a clown would do it, and get me attention besides.

At times I was humiliated because I was always lost when the teacher asked me to read. Kids can be cruel; it callouses you so that you start not caring about other people. I was in fear all the time at first, then I became calloused.

I had to choose a class of friends to stay protected. I always protected myself from people.

I was good at sports. But I could only go so far because my relationship with the kids on the teams could only get so close. I couldn't let them know about my lack of academic skills. If I let myself go all the way into their circle, they'd surely find out.

So I had to limit myself from total involvement in sports and with them. That put me around the kids that cut school and did mischievous things, and that was the start of my getting into trouble.

I was a fighter. During my recovery process, I learned that the times I saw my mom and dad fighting and then make up and become best friends were how I got the idea in my little sick mind that that's how you got to have best friends.

In my first year of high school, I started my stay at juvenile halls. During high school, I was basically incarcerated more time than not. So I was absent from school more than not.

I remember occasions when I was out twenty-seven or twenty-eight days [of school] out of thirty. I got further and further behind.

One time I really put forth some effort. I tried real hard to be good and get back on track, but the high school wouldn't take me back. They exempted me from all the schools in the county. Another time they took me back but only part-time.

Basically, I got to feel real safe and secure around others who couldn't read and write just like myself. So I felt best in institutions, with other human beings who couldn't be productive in society.

The result was that all but 18 months of my teenage life and half of my twenties was spent in institutions.[31] Believe me, I'll never say, "poor me." What I did was my choice.

Eventually I got to feel real safe and secure around others who couldn't read and write just like myself. So I felt best in institutions, with other human beings who couldn't be productive in society.

But who was I? Why was I? All I can say is by the grace of God I got a second chance around.

I was considered dangerous. I was a violent incarceree. People look at me now and don't believe it. Now I know the difference between how far I can go and how far I went before. I'm very content and happy.

I told my mother the other day I can't really remember any happy times as a child. It was stunning to her. Whatever bad I did, I meant to do. I was just very mischievous.

I guess I always had to be into something. It was because of the people I hung around with. They were always in trouble. They were always doing something bad, so I just wanted to do something a little more over the line, or a little more intense, to put me above them.

I can't really remember any happy times as a child.

In institutions you get taught the tricks of the trade—little ways to adapt to the environment there.[32] I look at myself back in San Quentin and Vacaville and realize that I'm no different from anyone that's there now. No, I believe it's because these people don't have other options and have nothing going for them academically.

I told my mother when she came to visit me in prison "I think I was put on this earth to be in and out of institutions." Basically I came to terms with that and I accepted it.

It took many years—five or six years later I started thinking I could've been wrong. There had to be something more than being locked up.

I just wanted to do something about myself. As the old saying goes, "When you get sick and tired of getting sick and tired, you do something about it." What it takes to get sick and tired I'll never know.

I didn't like the convicts I was around anymore. I don't know what happened, but all of a sudden I started disliking their conversations—what they talked about, what they were thinking, what they planned to do when they got out.

One day I thought, why get into even more trouble here? It doesn't make a whole lot of sense to keep fighting. That's how you got here, why keep it up?

When I got out each time for three or four months, I'd heard what other people had done while I was locked up. Then I'd go away again and wonder why I'm not doing those things.

I think I was put on this earth to be in and out of institutions.

But what *do* you do? You're young, no skills. Let's be honest, no one has made a big attempt to show what else could be an option for me. No one ever said to me, "Like if you get out and want to stay out this is what you do."

I don't remember anybody ever saying that. I don't remember anyone ever presenting it to me or giving me the idea.

Today I absolutely cannot believe that our correctional system is really serious about keeping people out of jail. I don't say everybody, but the majority of people in prison cannot compete and cannot be involved in society academically. They have no skills.

And you know what the scariest thing is? The budget cuts in education.

When we did *Nightline* together, Peter Waite from Laubach Literacy in New York said the nation was at great risk with the high illiteracy rate. There should be no price tag on education. I think we have our priorities mixed up.[33]

I said this to the newspaper I used to work for, and I think I expressed it well—"How can you expect to sell newspapers if you don't have readers?"

Soon they started supporting the literacy program.[34]

Now I go back to juvenile halls and give advice and the kids reject me as I rejected people telling me what to do.

I can look back today and honestly say that if I had taken 90% of their advice I'd never have been in trouble. Why didn't I? Because I wasn't ready. Also, when you're in that environment you have bad models.

I don't think the staff in the institutions care about the inmates. They're there for a job. They don't get involved in caring on a one-to-one basis.

Things started to get better for me. One day I saw an ad for a job at a newspaper. My wife helped me fill out the application. They hired me in the press room.

That job kept me out of trouble for awhile even though I was still on the edge. The problem was I still didn't know I was an okay person.

One day there was an ad in that paper for Project Second Chance. I contacted Second Chance and wound up with a tutor who wasn't working out well. She had to leave after awhile and my second tutor was a perfect match.[35]

I give advice to people entering programs: "Get the right teacher."

It's an emotional thing—we need support, we need to develop trust, we need to feel comfortable. There will be times when it is so frustrating.

I wanted to throw the book at times; I wanted to walk out. But if there's no pain there's no gain. The process of trying to digest the pain was good for me.

There were lots of positive things. I got to meet a lot of nice people and realized that I could talk to them,[36] that I could be comfortable around people and feel okay about myself, that there were things I had to say that people wanted to hear. I didn't have to be a clown.

I got invited on programs and that was the beginning of my speaking out. I learned to say okay to myself and let others know they're not the only ones who can't read or write, that it's okay to come out of the closet.

At literacy conferences I've seen people who've left their home town or county for the first time. There they meet hundreds of other real live people just like themselves who had admitted they couldn't read or write and done something about it.

There they learn that they're not alone, that they can feel safe. It seems that about the third day everyone starts to feel okay about being there.

When I speak at these literacy events, I try to make everyone feel comfortable right away so they can use this time together in the best possible way.

I try to throw out to them that before they know it, they'll be wishing they had more time with these people.

It's been eight years that I've really been okay. It's been uphill, but life is life.

I can work things through now, or find a way to laugh, knowing there's something positive at the end. It was hard to see this at the beginning of my recovery.

The bad years of my life—they've allowed me to touch others, to give something to others, and to be strong.

If I chose to say "poor me, my life was shattered. I lost so much."' I wouldn't be giving anything to anybody.

The only way I can possibly be strong, and understand, and be useful is to believe that things happen for a reason, some kind of in-depth reason that I don't understand. When I believe that what I went through has allowed me to touch someone else's life, then it was worth the trouble.

. . . the Youth Authority is just a prep school for the prison system . . .

A month ago I covered over the Hells Angels's tattoo with a rose. It used to mean a great deal to me. It was about a buddy I met at Vacaville, and went with to Soledad.

Now there's a peacock covering the KKK tattoo. The relief of not having them! That's another part of me being able to be released.

I'd really like to see all the official records of my past. When I was 21, waiting to get into prison for the first time, a doctor at Napa State Hospital recorded that I was a parasite, always taking and giving nothing in return.

They had a name they called me when I was growing up. "Crazy Bobby."

Why Must I Read?

Today, the blinders are away from my eyes and the chains are broken. Bobby is part of a world that he was very fearful of at one time. Today, I try to reach out to those who are still wearing the blinders and are chained to the illiterate world.

What can we do is the question. A lot, I say, but it won't be done overnight. We just can't limit ourselves. There just can't be a price tag on education. Whatever it takes is what we must do to move forward. Our great nation is at very serious risk and we must protect and defend our great nation at any cost. And there is a cost. Even a volunteer program like I was in takes money to staff and run in the best way possible.

Volunteers can do a lot, but they can't do it all. They too need help and that means money and funding. Because of my life's experience I feel that I can be a very positive force in helping people across the nation. I'm full of great ideas and suggestions and am eager to help in any way. I've been there! I know what it's like. I want to help others.

Excerpt from a piece Bob wrote which was published in a Project Second Chance newsletter.

How can you teach a kid to be caring and sensitive when they see the counselor brutalize and use strong force against other kids. Sometimes they have to, but sometimes it's abuse. I've seen counselors kick kids.

When you put a dog in the corner and kick it, it will bite you.

Darleen

They Don't Think It's Important

Darleen starts the interview by reading a new short story which is a tribute to her mother. An excerpt follows this statement.

Write! Because I want to. I write because I love it, about my family and friends and things close to me.

This one's about my granddaughter.

Here's another one about my mother. If I like a person, I'll just sit down and write about them.

I'm a student at Laney College in an intermediary program called Bridge. My family stood behind me 100%. Mother's always been an inspiration with everything in life, and my husband supports me in everything. He's my prime reason for reading.

A lot of people really won't take the time to help a person learning to read. My husband comes home from a busy day at work and sits down with me. He makes me want to learn to write even more things.

I didn't learn to read in school. I left school in 1970 to be there for my kids, but I always knew I'd go back. I never told my parents this or went to them for help. I guess I was really embarrassed. I remember making excuses about how I had to be here, had to be there.

Twenty years after I left school, after my kids were grown up, I realized I had a lot of problems with spelling. But when I read, the spelling comes to me. Now I can break the words down in my head and know what I'm doing. I've got confidence in myself.

When I write I don't really worry about the spelling as much anymore. I know it'll fall in place or I can always go back and correct it.

It's getting the main ideas down on paper that's important. When I write, I make a bunch of notes like a first draft. Then I'll go back, fix it up, add to it.

My original goal was to work with computers, but after seeing a lot of people who really need help, I want to be a teacher.

Yes, I want to teach reading to adults. I know how it is because I've been there. Maybe they can learn from my mistakes.

I have a teacher named Smokey Wilson at Laney in reading and writing. It's her first semester as a writing teacher, but she knows how to deal with her students and how to get her point across.

She's helped me break a lot of bad habits. I'd like to walk in her footsteps, she's my role model now. Maybe I can encourage my students to write.

When I was in school as a child, I was afraid of big words and tests. If I had told some teacher about my problem with not learning to read, maybe they would've embarrassed me. They might have made me sit up in front of the classroom.

I hesitated before I signed up at the writing classes. I was still scared, and I wondered what level the other students were at. But I knew then that if I had tackled reading, I could tackle anything.

I can recognize the reading problem in children who don't pick up books. If they're like I was, they don't think it's important.

I didn't pick up books, just played baseball and other sports all the time.

I couldn't read books to my children either. I wish I had been able to read to them. I think it's important. Fortunately my son reads really well. He's only fifteen, and he reads at college level.

I hope to bind up all of my writings.

I've written a story about my best friend Patricia Hill, whom I've gotten into the Berkeley Reads program.[37] She was looking for a tutor, but she didn't know where to go, so I told her. I found out through a friend too.

I feel that if you have a problem you should tell somebody about it. You shouldn't be scared to.

They can't help you if you don't let them know.

The One Person That I Most Admire

My mother went as far as the eighth grade in her formal education, but she didn't stop learning about life and what it had to teach her. She reads just about every newspaper article and magazines having to do with everyday happenings; and keeps up on sports and world events as well as the local changes we experience, both good and bad. She has taught me to be more aware of what's happening around me. Not just in my neighborhood but in my community as well; to listen and try to tell the difference in gossip and lies, and truth and fact, and how they might affect me.

We recently lost my brother Angelo after a long and painful illness. An uncle died but a few short weeks before him of complications following a severe heart attack. And my father was hospitalized for about four months with multiple problems; three separate times being returned to intensive care, we thought we would lose him each time. But through all of this while our family fretted and worried and stumbled around, mom kept everything and everyone together.

An excerpt from Darlene's story about her mother.

As One

As one we become;
two minds; two hearts; two loves.
together we flew
in love like the doves;
flirting and teasing
caressing and pleasing—we two.

as one we become;
two minds; two hearts; one love.
together we flew—
billing and cooing
nesting and wooing
mated together; we two.

as one we became;
four minds, four hearts; one love.
together we grow—
young hands and minds
holding and guiding
teaching and taught
life's struggles; fought—we too!

we learned and shared
we loved and cared;
our young grow up
and start on their own;
finding their hearts and loves
flying off; the new doves;
as one to become—we too!

CENSUS

Gene

You Don't Build a Pyramid Upside Down

When I was in the 7th grade, I asked a teacher why I couldn't read, what I had to do. She said I was going through a phase. I asked how long this phase would last. She said a short time.

I went back a year later, and she said the same thing. This lady was teaching in the school system until a year ago.

I have a 3rd grade education. I am unable to read in a normal way. But I've done literacy workshops in Kentucky for the federal government and asked if I have a Ph.D. in education. No, I just memorize.

It's very hard for people to understand when they find out a person who is doing a regular job can't read or write.

I can identify illiterate people anywhere.

In class they copy identically what the teacher writes as notes. If the teacher underlines or crosses out a word, so will they. When I go on speaking engagements across the country, I use a little test we devised to detect the illiterates.

We give very specific instructions to the audience, like exactly how to fill out the application form. Only the illiterates will do it right because they listen very carefully to everything you say. That's how we know them.

These people aren't stupid, but attain their information by memory. Since they cannot function by reading, they found another way. An individual who can't read depends on recall from his own brain, like a computer.

They key in everything. It's the way we have learned to survive.

This recall is much more advanced in illiterates than others. I could take a car apart, and tell you how each part would function, and put it back together.

Being illiterate doesn't mean you aren't intelligent.

An engineer at NASA memorized every component part of a missile. A stockbroker memorized what comes across the board, Sammy Davis Jr. memorized his lyrics.

This is hard to believe. You have to ask, "Are these people for real?"

Depictions in airports and public buildings for non-readers are there because people need to understand some things, whether they read and write or not. A few years ago, it was realized that there were more of these people around than anyone had thought.

It takes me a full night to read the funny pages, but I was the president of a credit union. I helped train Great America (now Wells Fargo) personnel in their banking. Some of the instructions I put together talking into a machine are now in print and still being used. I sat on the Board of the credit union Advisory Council.

People still call me for help. The people I helped never knew I was illiterate. Now I'm asked how I could give out data and information.

I answer, "Because I dealt with it every day. Being illiterate doesn't mean you aren't intelligent."

I made a hieroglyphic dictionary. If you looked at it you could tell exactly what the words meant. I gave it to the Department of Education, and they're planning on putting it in the Smithsonian.

I was a modification engineer for Caterpillar. I was asked, "How is this possible that you can teach engineering concepts to people?"

My answer, "The people who taught me showed me."

My wife helped me interpret memos or modification instructions. She was an avid reader. She didn't know it, but she was my eyes. I would ask her not only to read but what it was about.

When my wife became blind, I had to learn to read. My wife couldn't believe it. She thought I just couldn't spell.

She didn't know it,
but she was my eyes.

She asked, "Do you mean to tell me that since we were married you couldn't read?"

"How did you drive across country?"

"How did you get certified with a first-class truck driver's license?"

My kids couldn't believe I couldn't read. They asked me how I could've helped them with essays.

They didn't know it took me a half hour to write a regular sentence with a dictionary. I'd stay up all night to read their homework. My ultimate goal then was to read the *National Geographic* to understand what the pictures were about.

Now I speak out across the country. I focus on elementary and junior high school because I want to give back something for those who taught me early on.

I tell these kids the definition of a dummy is "one who cannot operate in certain ways." Illiterates take a little longer to process things, but once they do it's like a computer. Their brain has become a computer so advanced that it is capable of incredible things.

I say, "Don't stop at the door."

"What you've already learned in that way is important."

"You are unique."

When you develop reading along with this skill you will have a memory bank and storage bank that is almost unlimited. You can advance to any level you want. We are different, let's not lose this ability we've developed over the years.

Now I'm a federal officer. I'm a scale technician and director of training for the Department of Weights and Measures.

The person who trained me didn't realize I couldn't read until we were working with a manual. He was the first person to find out.

When he found out I was giving workshops, he warned me that if anyone else found out I'd be in real trouble. He told me I would have to explain all of my director's jobs. He told me I was going to have to learn to read.

I was scared.

It was the most frightening thing that had ever happened. I avoided him because he found out something I had hidden from everyone for years.

Before that I was an instructor first-class for wiring the warheads of missiles and Nikes. I realized at that point that my 3rd grade reading skills were not going to carry me through life.

Years before, in college, I functioned in groups of ten or twelve. I couldn't take notes in class, so I would always make sure I was the last to regurgitate what the others had reported.

I was the one who would sum it all up, but only after I'd gotten the information from them. I could tell you who said what, the process, the meaning, what had taken place, and the final outcome.

Mrs. Bush did a great justice to illiterates to put herself in their corner with her backing and support.

I got good grades, never a problem I had to function this way to keep ahead of everyone else. I could goof off though because I had this talent.

I used to scribble nonsense that looked like I was taking notes in class. I got so used to this that I still do it when I hear someone lecture.

My intelligence and memory was both good and bad. They allowed me to function, but not to learn how to read. It got so that I couldn't ask people to teach me to read.

In junior high school I got good grades and didn't have to work hard at it. I even goofed off. I wasn't a problem child in school.

I realize now that I had to keep ahead of everybody. I always volunteered to extra-curricular things.

Mrs. Bush did a great justice to illiterates to put herself in their corner with her backing and support. When I met her for the first time, I told her I couldn't believe no one had come forward before.

She told me they hadn't, "because nobody wants to come forward and say they know illiterates." No one wants to put themselves per se into that category.

At the workshops I conducted, I handed out flyers for Project Read. I had no idea at the time that I would have to go to them for help.

It took me a month to call them for myself. When I did call for an appointment, the response I got was, "Are you sure you're here as a student and not a tutor?"

They just wouldn't believe me and tried to convince me I was there to be a tutor. Here's this guy I come to for help.

I say, "Look, I can't read, I can't write, I can't do normal function things."

I was humiliated.

I never expected to go back.

When I see him now he says that he still can't believe that he put me through what he did.[38] This kind of thing still happens everywhere, continuously.

When I talk to tutors now, I tell them they have to work one-to-one with these people to help them come out of their shell. It's very hard for them to say they can't function like a human being.

Non-readers feel they are 3rd class citizens. 2nd class citizens have some abilities and functions that they can do. For example, when I scribbled my notes, people thought, "This guy's got his act together. "Ask him a question, and he's got the answer."

It was a life of copying.

But inside I knew I wasn't functioning.

I carried with me at all times for 12 years, day and night, a pocket tape recorder the size of a miniature radio. It recorded everything I heard.

In the workshops I conducted, when questions came up I needed to refer back and plug it into my brain. When the question came up again I wanted to be able to answer quickly, sensibly and without hesitation.

My recorder helped me with directions. When people write them out, they speak them out loud as well. When I'd hear the instructions a second time, I'd memorize them.

Like my wife all over again, talking to me. Written words meant nothing to me. I would match the information marked down against the words on the machine and find streets, deliver materials, "read" invoice messages and instructions.

It was a life of copying. These are the kinds of things an illiterate person does. These are the kinds of functions they maintain.

I've seen engineers who couldn't read the blueprints, a lathe operator who couldn't read the instructions. And they did their jobs well. What irritates me now is when employers find they have employees who are illiterate and want to let them go.

Half a dozen of us have been traveling cross country talking to corporations about this—Ford, GM—there are about 20 companies on my list. John Corcoran is one of us. We've come into the limelight.

They come to us now mostly, but I also call them. I get to them through the PR departments. I tell them, "This is who we are, and this is what we do. Let us in."

We ask to speak at conventions. We make them aware of what's going on in their own house. We give advice about personnel with reading problems to administrators, shop people, teachers.

I show them how they can utilize the two years or more worth of training they have already invested in these people and amortize this investment.

Make it a volunteer situation on a one-to-one basis without embarrassment, shame, or fear. Then that individual will bring others into the system.

It works.

Before they got only 60% from that employee, now they get 100%. SONY has found success with employees who have worked 10-20 years, valuable employees.

Now they're saying "Why didn't we see this sooner."

You don't build a pyramid upside down.

Yvette

It Took Me Longer...To Grow Up

Yvette is a large, jovial woman with a round expressive face and a prevailing sense of humor.

It will take me twelve years to become certified as a psychiatrist. I started last Monday after years of preparation. I had to learn how to read. The reading will still be the biggest problem in school with the heavy technical reading loads but should get easier, and then the frustration with it should let up, as time goes on.

My counselor is hanging in there, encouraging me. I expect to make it, even though one of my counselors a few years ago thought it was unrealistic for someone like me.

You see it took me longer than most people to grow up. I was raised as an imbecile. Sometime about age six I was diagnosed as dyslexic.

Dyslexia wasn't very well understood then, and there weren't many places you could go to for help. My parents kept it a secret. They never told me what was wrong, just treated me specially, like a total dependent with no hope for the future.

My younger sister took on my role as the eldest and had to help raise the younger children and me. She resented this then and even more now that I've turned out okay. She's the one who finally told me about my problem. Everyone did for me. I got used to it.

In the fourth grade I left regular school and went into special ed, then on to vocational school, where they teach you how to eventually get around barriers—like reading for example. You learn to avoid situations where reading is necessary.

So I became an introvert all through growing up. In high school the teachers gave me a free hand for the first time and encouraged me to become more independent.

They offered me the opportunity to be an exchange student even though I didn't know any foreign language. I did it anyway, and it was fun. I was on my way.

I signed up for a literacy program at Mission Jr. College in preparation for going there. It cost $5 per class, two nights a week for two years. There was no enthusiasm on the part of the teacher. I didn't learn much there.

On my own I went to a doctor at age 26. Diagnosed dyslexic again, I did therapy for two years to the point of being cross-eyed, which was progress, but I stopped, discouraged.

A little while later I started seeing eye doctors and was told that surgery was needed and there was a 50-50 chance between correcting the cross eyes and blindness. I decided to go for it, and before I did, mother told me about a literacy program in a junior college she'd seen on TV. The surgery worked.

So then I went to sign up for the literacy program. It's embarrassing. You see, because everybody always did for me.

When I went to sign up at the junior college, I took my teacher, my mother, the lady from the work experience program I was in, all with me. My mom had always taken me everywhere, even to Social Security to get my benefits, because I was HANDICAPPED. It's degrading.

It was hard to get out of it, but I look back and see that I could've done it earlier than I did; so many people were there to help me get on my own way.

Now I'm very independent.

Independence came finally when I got a job and my own apartment in 1982. My mom helped me find the way, through the social services. It was difficult for her and for me to break the old cycle. We are not co-dependents any longer.

It took a lot of growing up and change for both of us, and a separation. My mom had to develop her own life. She had a hard time learning to let go, she wanted to keep a hold on me. I live with her now again, but it's very different from before.[39]

When Paul, my tutor, gave me an assignment to write about the program I got very emotional. What I wrote got published two times in newsletters and in *The Drum* book of new readers' works.

I'll continue to write for my personal self—diaries, journals, jot down thoughts—I think my first journal was in 1982.

I still get frustrated.

I try to use big words and don't always spell them right. I still feel like throwing books against the wall now and then.

My life has changed so much that I don't know where to start. I'm learning how not to be afraid of reading. Last week I took a test and with a little help I passed. I took the same test last year. I was unable to read it and did not pass. . . . Before I decided to get into this reading program, I had told myself that I could get by without really knowing how to read. Then one day I realized that all my friends that I worked with were taking tests to get promoted to new jobs.

Excerpted from a story Yvette wrote.

Sidney

I Wanted To Be An Educated Person

Sid is 43, a high school graduate with approximately 45 college units who reads at a fourth grade level. He is a Vietnam combat vet and a recovering alcoholic. At the beginning of the interview, he reminisces about his mentor grandfather who won Olympic medals and taught himself to read Latin.

Only this summer did I find out, in tests for learning disabilities, that I had "processing" defects in my brain. That means when I hear an instruction, it goes around a different circuit. From what I understand it has nothing to do with intelligence, it just takes me longer.

Now I remember, as a kid I could never understand why I had so much trouble. I could read a word but never could spell it.

I always did well in classes where I didn't have to read and write. I had a history class that I got B's in because the teacher read to us. In shop classes I always got straight A's. That's why I wanted to be a machinist.

One of my papers as an adult student was about my learning difficulties as a kid and the whole process of educating myself. It all started in about the 3rd grade. Then, when I had just turned 12 my dad died. Mom wasn't in such good shape, so she sent three of us off to boarding school and kept the youngest one at home.

I was sent to the Christian Brothers. They were abusive. I felt deserted by my mother and trapped in a prison-like situation right in the middle of Berkeley. It was a hostile situation where absolutely no attention was given to possible problems.

I wasn't doing well in school. I was considered a discipline problem—goofing off—so I got whippings for it. As a kid, I felt, "I'm innocent, I didn't do anything wrong, I couldn't help it if I didn't get an A." I still harden back to that time as critical in my education.

I got stuck in the dummy classes.

My sister had a college education because mom was reverse macho. She felt the boys could always make a living digging ditches, it's the girl who needs an education. I got stuck in the dummy classes, then later, in high school in remedial reading class.

When I'm in my most cynical moods, I say I am a product of a 60s education—I can't read or write, but I was passed through school as long as I showed up.

I was even given a high school diploma and 55 units of college credits. I'm a machinist. If I could've read and written better, I would've chosen another life.

Now I feel that if you could just communicate what you're feeling and your thoughts by putting it down—straight from the head to the paper—then anything is possible.

At the time, a young man aged 18 or 19, unmarried and without a job, joined the marines.[40] In the infantry I learned how to fire various weapons, but I never got into the learning classes that I'd hoped to get into.

Maybe it's because I didn't score high enough in the various tests they gave me. My highest score was in electronic communications, because I could distinguish between dots and dashes I guess. My second highest score was in general infantry.

I was in a real crazy state of mind after serving 17 months, 27 days in Vietnam. I have to say that drugs and alcohol got involved here. I was talking to my therapist the other day about this.

In the frame of mind I was in then, a real macho young man, full of patriotism and all that John Wayne stuff, I didn't realize the insanity of what was going on over there.

I don't want to make a political statement, but I went from the far right to the far left on this. Now I'm back to the right, and I think we might have had a reason to be there, but the whole process had gotten really screwed up. A lot of guys died for nothing as far as I'm concerned.

I got out with a physical disability; I'm blind in one eye, and I don't hear too well. When I got out, I bummed around and sat around and finally got a job which required a 4-year apprenticeship. It was blue collar type training, but required a lot of reading. This was a problem.

I worked there for ten years and got into trouble—drugs and alcohol. This got progressively worse. In December of 1981 I was arrested for drunk driving for the fourth time. The judge put it to me "Whether you admit it or not, it's apparent you have a drinking problem. Either you're going to stop, or I'm going to stop you. Suspended, as long as you attend a ninety-day drinking/driving program."[41]

I have thoughts and opinions that pop up that I'd like to report.

I had to take antiabuse for six-months. It's a drug which simulates a heart attack if you drink. It makes you violently ill so you think you're going to die. It doesn't change your behavior, but it does make you stop drinking. They make you break up these pills into little pieces and put into something and eat it. Then it was AA.

In therapy, we got into my life. I learned that I had a pretty good brain, but it never worked for me. I had never learned how to get out there and deal with the world on the world's terms.

In therapy I looked at my stressed out, frantic mother. She was always on the edge of a breakdown trying to raise us kids alone. My father's death when I was twelve. Vietnam. My friends who died for nothing.

In the process of quitting drinking and therapy, I started thinking about what I still can do about my life. The answer was to go back to school.

I joined a program called the Reading Game[42] with eight-year olds because even though my reading comprehension and vocabulary tested at 12.9 (college level), my reading skills were on the 5th grade level.

It was kind of embarrassing being a 35-year old in that class. But it worked!

I went on with the Literacy Plus program. I went to remedial classes, then a class in writing as a prerequisite for regular college English classes. I wanted to be what I call an educated person—to read and write proficiently.

I had decided to start with the writing. It had always been in my head to write books and journals and criticism. I have thoughts and opinions that pop up that I'd like to report.

In my therapy and study of psychology, I read that Jung said that if most people worked at keeping a good journal they wouldn't need therapy. That's true. When I write I find that I get a lot of therapy. I like how my head works, but it's like pulling teeth to get it out of there.

I as a child, like most people, had a very active imagination and had an entirely different existence in my fantasy world from my real world. In this world everyone intuitively knew what I wanted and needed and most importantly, agreed with me. They loved me for me, not for what I might do for them or give to them. Of course they all saw my absolutely flawless wisdom and logic. The world according to me, by me, and for me, was good for all as far as I was concerned. This fantasy world was okay for a child, but at the age of 16, I found alcohol, and I liked it from the start. I also found that under the effects of alcohol I felt good, as good as I did in my fantasy world. There was the start of using first alcohol, then later drugs, to alter, therefore make acceptable, my experiences of life. This all worked well enough in my early years, before I lost my ability to control my drinking and using. By my early thirties, my life was in a sad state of affairs. I knew that things had to change. I knew that things had to change, even though I didn't quite know how these changes were to come about. These changes in my life were going to come about with or without my consent.

. . . Then there is the money I had wasted on drugs and alcohol, which I estimate to be in excess of $30,000 over the years. As bad as all these were, the worst was the endless loneliness I felt in those years. Life wasn't working for me anymore. In fact I felt that life was passing me by. To quote a verse of song I used to like, I was "Looking for love in all the wrong places." I was living in an illusion that life, love, and happiness would just happen to me.

Excerpt from an essay Sid wrote for an English class.

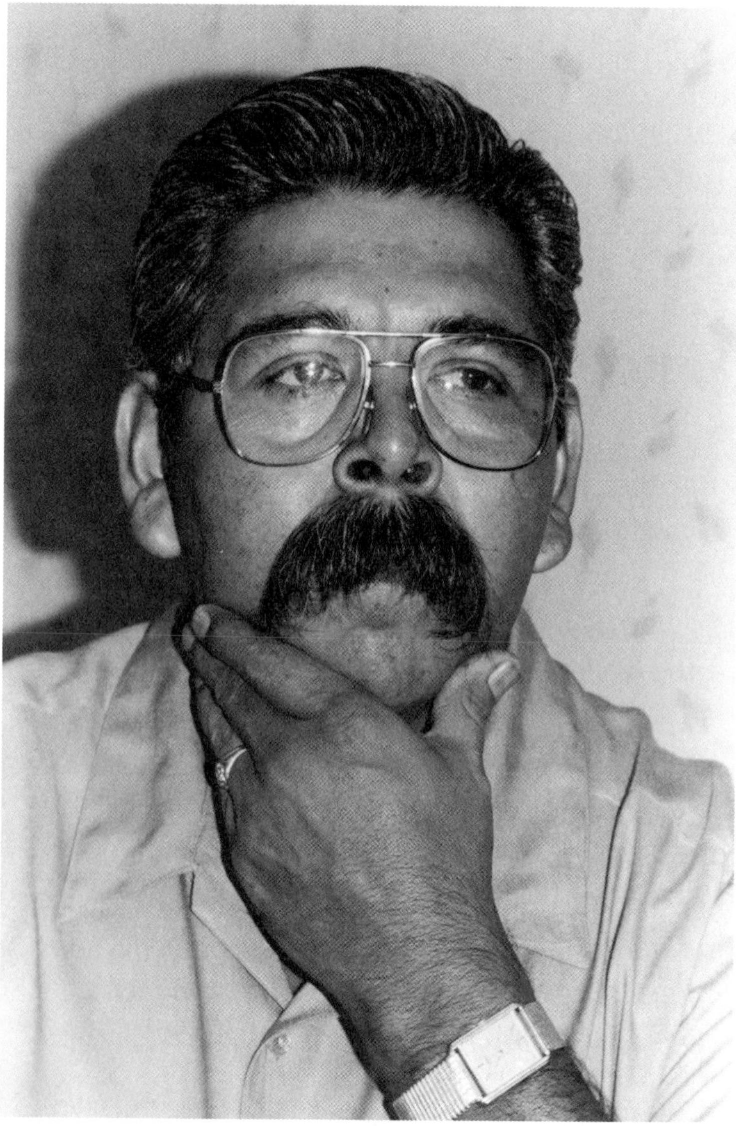

Sam

Did You Ever Learn How To Read, Sam?

Sam was raised by his grandparents and spoke English only in school, which he attended until the ninth grade.

My reason for not learning how to read was because my grandparents wouldn't allow me to speak English at home. I was only allowed to speak Spanish so they could understand me. I think that's where my downfall all started, because without much English, school wasn't interesting to me.

I just went, and learned not to lose face. I threw my homework to my cousin who did it for me. The teachers just passed me along from grade to grade. In the 7th grade I came here to Sante Fe Springs to live with my mother.

That's where things got real hard; I didn't have anyone to do my work for me and things got even more difficult. They put me into a "continuation" school, which means half the day you go to school and half the day you work.

As I got older, I started to get into trouble all the time. Went to jail and fell even more behind. Got jobs, mostly warehouse work, and it started getting more and more embarrassing because people started noticing that I didn't know how to read.

I started learning how to hide it. I started to believe that they were becoming more and more sophisticated about detecting it. Maybe this part was just coming from inside me and not really true at all.

When I had a job driving a tow truck, I memorized the streets and landmarks to find my way around. When I "read" a newspaper, I could always pick up bits and pieces. And people thought I was reading.

Even my wife didn't know I couldn't read. When I did finally tell my wife she was surprised. She said, "But I've seen you reading the newspaper." She works at a school, and her mother is a language assessor. They are well educated people.

I came to feel inferior and to feel bad. Didn't feel like a man.

One of the reasons I had to tell my wife was that I had gotten laid-off at this time and had to bring her around with me to fill out job applications.

I sought out Jerry (the director) at the literacy program then and kept up the program for three months. I found a new job at a travel agency, then went to work for the Builders Emporium. When they put me on a night shift, I had to stop the literacy program for about a year. When I went on disability, I came back to the program. I've been in it a total of seven months.

My goal is to be able to pick up a newspaper and read it from beginning to end. I think, no, I KNOW, I would better myself if I could read.

For example, I'm involved with a youth group at church—ages 13 to 21—which tries to keep them out of trouble. Some listen when I tell my story. Some are hard core, don't believe, don't listen.

I want to get them out of the street, get them off drugs. 75% are on drugs, the others are toying with the idea. We're trying to get their lives back together. The kids are from all over.[43]

We started with ten kids from the church and invited them for a weekend. The next time they brought more kids. Now there are 250 with only about 10 counselors. It keeps growing. We serve lots of food from morning to night, every day each weekend.

I got involved with them after speaking before a group of about 100 people about my reading progress and aspirations. A woman present asked me if I wanted to join the church youth program.

I tell these kids that I can't read. Right away they ask me why.[44]

They say, "Didn't you go to school?"

I say, "Yes."

I've thought so many times, since I can remember, that I could never do it—read. But I've had so many challenges in my life and taken them, that one day I decided to take reading as a challenge too.

What started it off was my 20th high school reunion. Although I never graduated from high school, I got invited to this, and a girl who had been assigned to tutor me in reading in the 9th grade came up to me and asked, "Did you ever learn how to read Sam?"

I turned around and wanted to die. Being the honest person I am, I said, "No, I never learned." That started it off I guess.

I had really made up my mind before I signed up. When I learn to read better, I would put myself into school to learn counseling. That's a good three years away, but I'll do it.

I've got the experience; and, well, I know I'll do it. There's no back alley I haven't walked.

Linda

My Writing Is Broadening My Aspect of Me

Linda is a bouncy person who uses language to do all sorts of things she aims for. Within a week of this interview Linda will be moving to Richmond. There she intends to pursue writing seriously. She is assertive, well-spoken with a strong southern accent, knows what she wants and articulates clearly how she will get there. We're rooting for her.

I've always known how to read, never had a literacy problem. The reason I got involved in the literacy program was to brush up on my skills[45] so I could go back to college. I needed to learn how to function in a classroom again.

I'm getting into writing again and found it interesting there because there were a number of other writers in the program, as tutors. My tutor is a very educated man, and he helped me with my English so much that I was writing good poems. I got all of them together and wanted to start looking for a publisher.

Then he encouraged me to write short stories. I have ten of them now, but my format and my English aren't correct. I've been out of college too long. What I think about, and what I want to do, is to learn more English before I go ahead with the short stories.

My writing is broadening my aspect of me. By looking at myself and putting it on paper, I see where I've been, and where I need to go. I'm a descriptive writer. It gives me a cleaner, broader look. I didn't know this would happen when I entered the literacy program.

The other people recognized that I could write. My tutor and other people in the program said "Look, you're a good writer, if you continue with your English and your format you can go a long way."

I just want people to get something from me being a writer.

I always knew I was a bright person, and I know I had an art for writing. In high school I had taken up journalism but never did finish. But this time around it made me feel as if I was worth something, that I was one of those writers who could get down what people are feeling, who could express on paper what they can't say.

Like if you want to be brought up to be joyous and happy, I write about birds and animals and comical things. For children, I write happy children's stories. Or if you want to be serious, I'll write about kids' behavior, kids in classrooms, etc.

I'm not the type of writer that's looking for a lot of money. I just want people to get something from me being a writer. Do you know what I mean?

When I was seven I used to write and fantasize. What I dreamed about didn't come true, but it was a better way than what was real. It kept me going then.

My fantasy life kept me going. I didn't have friends. The writing kept me going. It me feel good. It still does.

When I write something funny I laugh. When I write sad things I get distressed.

The child never grew out of me until I was 28 years old. That was after AA recovery.[46]

At 17 I got onto drugs. Because of a bad relationship I took some PCPs and ended up in a psychiatric facility.

When I got older, I got a little wiser, and got more realistic after I stopped using and started writing again.

The writing helped me do it. I have a lot of journals I

wrote through the worst times. Sometimes I feel sad when I read through them. Sometimes they give me the chills.

My parents lost hope. They didn't want anything to do with me. Now my sister's taking her turn in trouble, maybe even going to lose her kid because of it.

Now I see all the trouble I put them through because it's like what she's causing my parents now. I understand now, being sober.

My husband, common law, was with me all through this, and he went through hell. It makes me sad now because I put age on him.

When we met he was 26, and he looked 17. Now he's 36, and he looks 47. I went through hell, and I'm still going through it, but I can handle it.

I've been out two years, and I've used only two times.

Soon I'll be moving away from my mother. As much as I love her, she's no good for me because she's an alcoholic.

When I'm alone, I can concentrate on the writing. I've been a loner all of my life. When I'm to myself, that's when I get the right vibes about what I want to do.

I'd like to go back and read the old writers, black writers, all kinds of writers, and capture what they wrote about back then, twenty or thirty years, and compare it with new writers—how we feel and what we think is going on in society. Where we've been and where we're going.

I read and absorb a lot about people, and observe. I'm a descriptive writer. I've been invited to a conference for Black Writers.

After I move I'm going to go. I'm going to go for it.

Just for Today

Just for Today
Just for today I feel peace
Just for today I am listening to me
Just for today I have a friend
A friend to me that lives deep within
Just for today I can walk in the breeze
Just for today I can easily feel pleased
for the things I do. I can smile and say
Yes, just for today God has kept me
in a peaceful and clean way.
I'm presently living through a clean mirror
in a more dignified way.
Yes, that is how I am living
Just for Today.

Having Hope

Don't know where I've been;
Don't know where I want to go;
Don't know why the sun fades to black at night;
Don't know why the sun lights the day

All these reasons why: I don't know
But one thing I Do Know!
I'm here on this Earth;
in this universe,
with the fear that finds the darkness
and listens to its sound.
The sound of yesterday fears
Having in some shape, form–or
fashion–of scars left in me.

Paul

A Flame That Burns Inside Within Me

Between birth and age 17 I'd been in 27 foster homes. The last one, number 28, gave me the foundation that was the beginning of my life.

Five years ago, they diagnosed me as dyslexic, but as early as the third or fourth grade, they put me into special ed.

By my junior year in high school I had built up my reading skills to college level and got two scholarships. One was to the Cordon Bleu School in Paris for cooking and I accepted.

But just before I left I was in a terrible car accident right in front of my school. A cop was chasing some guy who was speeding. The guy hit me.

I fell and got up dazed just in time to have the cop's car hit me. I was hurt pretty badly and spent months in the hospital.

Before the accident I was athletic and won trophies. Many years later, during the riots in Sacramento, I watched my high school burn down with my trophies inside.

When I recovered I went to Paris and was pampered there. But I was worried all the time because my memory was deteriorating. I couldn't remember recipes I loved and started having trouble doing math and with reading.

By the time I came home two years later, reading was gone completely. The doctors couldn't understand why language stayed with me. They say it's irreversible, but I don't accept that. I challenge it.

I've had so many doors close on me, so many ups and downs, that I don't let this bother me, won't allow myself to be daunted by it.

When someone says, "No," I say, "Yes." My therapist says I have a flame that burns inside within me, sometimes it only flickers or wiggles, but I won't let it go out.

I developed a way of reading by learning the small words and guessing the big ones. It worked, but not well enough. I lost opportunities for lots of jobs I applied for because I couldn't read well enough.

Now I'm learning to read again, but have to go over my lessons six or more times. If I leave them alone for a couple of days, I'm confused. I know that I can never let up, or I'll deteriorate back down to where I was before.

I'm old, can't afford to lose time.

To develop discipline, to work hard instead of scream or lash out—that's the way I feel about life.

When June [his tutor] asked me to write about myself, I saw it as an opportunity. She had to help me with the spelling, but the words came pouring out. A voice came from inside.

I want to write more, to speak out, not to be angry but to do something about real human problems.

Once, only a year ago, I was at the brink of suicide after living in the shelter eight years and all. At the medicine section of the grocery store, I opened a bottle of something I knew was poison and started guzzling it down.

A stranger, a lady, knocked it out of my hand. And when the druggist came and asked her if I was bothering her, she said "No, he just knocked this bottle off a shelf."

She drove me to Valley Medical Center. They put me in an observation room. Then—and this part I can't relate to—the doctor says, "You don't have to go back to the shelter if you promise me you won't hurt yourself."

And he shelled out $165 for a private room with a TV for a night. I said to myself, "After all these years trying to figure out how to get somewhere, now this, ha!"

So I promised not to hurt myself. Then the next day they sent me to Valley Medical for help.

I tried to figure out what I was going to tell them there—how every time I tried hard things got worse; and when I did bad it got better.

I was lying there thinking, what's next?

Then a weirdo comes to my door, bangs on the door, makes a lot of noise.

The cops come. Instead of taking him away, they make *me* leave my room. I go out into the street and start to walk.

The cops come after me then, and say they had made a mistake, and I could go back to my room.

I did, then lied down, turned off the TV, closed the blinds, wouldn't be disturbed. I had a migraine headache, took pills that didn't work but only made me more depressed.

It was Christmas Eve. The next day I went to the mission for Christmas breakfast. A fight breaks out next to me, and I get hit with a tray, food all over me.

Then I went to church, the only safe place, and stayed there for the weekend, two whole days. I knew on Monday morning I could go back to Valley Medical.

When I did get there the guy at the reception desk told me first thing I had to fill out some papers.

This was right after I told him I had trouble reading words. So then I told him I'd just had a nervous breakdown. He let me in.

I met Diane Hayward there, she's an internist.

I told her how many times I'd had to tell my story—to the General Assistance people...and how tired I was of repeating it, how I felt like a folder being opened and closed over and over like my story wasn't interesting enough the first time, like history wasn't good enough, like "Let's have a better one this time."

I told her I had trouble reading words. She listened. She's been a lot of help.

I try to help too. I'm an expert on welfare, been on it since I was two.

I've lived in homeless shelters[47] for eight years, all over. I've lived for years on $38 a month food stamps and know how to make deals exchanging work for room and board (like the time I did cooking part-time at a residents club). So I'm able to give all kinds of people advice. Food stamps, G.A. (general assistance), part time jobs.

When I lived in a shelter in San Jose, I used to walk over the bridge that that famous community of homeless lived under.

One day I got curious enough and went down there under the bridge. I thought, this is bizarre, these people live here.

I told them I knew where people could get help. At first they didn't trust me but I started slowly making friends with them, gaining their confidence.

I told them how to get around the state requirement to have an address—just get a letter mailed to them at some address!

I told them that if I got caught telling them these things, I'd get into trouble, but that my system works.

I also told them about the scam, where the shelter collects $172 from the government out of a needy person's welfare check just for giving you a bed, leaving you with only $26 for everything else.

My goal is to write a manual for homeless kids[48] and adults about getting around in the system.

Martin Luther King has been a big influence on my life ever since my grandmother, who was a missionary, took me to Alabama for the marches when I was a tiny little boy. This has always given me strength.

I also want to write something about reaching out. Instead of getting angry, I'd like to say "Let's do something about it."

The Hard Knocks

The hard knocks that I go through like being in line for food, trying to find a phone to use, never having enough money to do laundry, getting the run around, and trying not to get depressed about everything, I somehow always read inside of me. I look at the flame in my heart that's burning to see how it grows because it's my only way of knowing that I'm still a part of society when I'm at my lowest point. It makes me want to go on.

Since the interview, Paul is no longer homeless and has moved into a board and care home, then into his own apartment. He is engaged to a young women he met at college where he is now enrolled in classes. He works hard for literacy. Paul is an example of a learner who has empowered himself and others.

Maria

Otherwise You Are Nothing, I Think

Maria began her studies at the Commerce Public Library literacy program and transferred to Project Life in Santa Fe Springs Public Library in 1988. Her natural boyancy and determination have allowed her to overcome serious medical problems, including a kidney transplant, in recent years. She views writing as important to survival, in many ways.

I was born in Tijuana, Mexico and learned to read and write in Spanish. I came to America at age 14 and married an Hispanic man when I was 24.

We lived in the City of Commerce. I went to the municipal pool to swim and there was a poster advertising a reading program.

Before that I had studied English a little by myself, but I wanted to write and speak in a correct way.[49] I signed up, and they provided me with a tutor within a week.

We met in a park. There were four in our group of students. I was too scared to ask questions at first and too shy to ask for help. But the tutor was a caring and sensitive person who wanted to learn about us.

She worked us hard, gave us writing assignments for homework over the weekend. We met once a week.

After she found out my dream was to have something published, she printed my story and gave me the little book at my graduation from level II at City Hall.

I was so shocked, so very happy. I wrote that story while under dialysis for kidney failure, a four-hours long procedure, a four-hours long story.

The nurse read it first, and she was surprised that it was such a happy story.

I wanted to learn computers. A long time ago, when I knew just a few English words, I went to a place to learn.

They told me I had to know better English first. Now I'm almost ready to go back there. I also wanted to pronounce words properly and to help myself solve problems.

I wanted to be able to write answers back to the credit companies[50] when they send their threatening letters through the mail.

Now I feel so great. I can answer back. I can write credit companies back that if you pay your bills on time, they have no right to threaten you. To others as well, I can answer back.

Sometimes people are cruel. Today I feel secure because nobody puts me down anymore. I can defend myself. Before I couldn't. I wanted to but I couldn't speak the language.

Now I see people on the street, or in a store, who need help translating. Even if they don't ask, I can see them looking around for help.

I help young people, old people. Then I tell them about the literacy program. If they say they're too old, I tell them it's no excuse.

I say the important thing is to want to learn. I tell them the program isn't going to get up and walk to you. Some people like to be dependent though.

Not me.

I'm a fighter, don't let things put me down. Life is hard. You will always have something there to stop you. You've got to keep going. Otherwise you are nothing, I think.

August 28, 1990

Dear Governor Deukmejian:

My name is Maria Gutierrez and it is important to me and other people to continue having the literacy program (Bill #AB3381) in our community because it is a program that is very helpful for adults. We learn so much with this program. I am a student since 1985 and I am so proud having this program in our state.

Please help us and support us by continuing to have this program here and everywhere people need it because it is very important for all Americans who can't read or write.

Thanks for your help.

Caryl Richards Representative
Faberge Incorporated

Dear Sir:

The reason I write this letter is to ask you why you do not put this product in the market anymore.

I've used this shampoo and condition for 15 years and it is hard for me to start using another product. I have a real sensitive nose and I get easily a headache smelling other products....If you are not going to continue putting your product in the market anymore will you please tell me how I can get it from you through the mail?

Yours truly

a desperate customer

John

It's About The Joy Of Learning Something

Because John is making a career of his accomplishments in literacy, he has become a controversial and much talked about figure among adult literacy educators and other professionals. As a college graduate, former teacher, and successful businessman before he entered a literacy program, he has been widely interviewed in the media. His story seems so unreal—can this be true?

When I was a child during World War II, I saw the literate world as Nazis. I, illiterate, saw myself as a Jew, and I had to hide.

As a child I was happy, but not in school. It was a terrible place. I had to be on guard all the time. I graduated from the University of Texas, El Paso. Had four National Science Foundation grants: one of them was for sociology and economics at Santa Clara University. This was the best course I ever had in my life, got a legitimate "A" in it because it was based on interaction and had no reading and no writing. Two others were for San Diego State; and the last was at LSU for sociology and economics. This last was the best experience I ever had. Didn't have to do any reading, all interaction. I couldn't read.

The article in *Esquire* made my story believable to me. I came to the library to learn how to read, not to be on TV or in magazines or be interviewed.

We think there's something wrong with us, especially those of us who've been through the school system. We think something is wrong with our brain, and we've been taught that's why we didn't learn to read.

I don't like the term "reading disabilities." I think this is part of the problem. In retrospect, I'm one of those people. Now that I am learning how to read, I'm fascinated with the inner workings of my brain, what the problems were.

My 13 months with a tutor just taught me to de-code and made me able to read things like *Time* Magazine. I was highly motivated to read the *Esquire* article about me, but it's on a level that's still challenging for me.

So I've learned to communicate, but I'm still on a 4th to 5th grade level in spelling. It will take me 10-years to resolve the whole problem and know how to read. After all, it took me 40 years to develop my oral skills, and with literacy training, these are improving too.

In America there are two languages and two cultures. First is the oral, the language of a primitive tribe. The second is written. Now I feel bilingual in a sense. I can communicate in this new language and belong to this new culture.

The only cure for illiteracy is literacy.

But I thought it would take me 5 years to get over the emotional trauma of being an illiterate in this society. Now I want to push that up to 7 years, in terms of healing because I'm in my 4th year now, and I still break down and cry.

The healing that has to take place involves the low self-esteem that goes together with illiteracy. I've been speaking publicly for three years about this. It's been a catharsis, cheaper than a psychiatrist.

The first phase humbled me. It's about the joy of learning something.

To be illiterate in America today is a form of child neglect. I believe that all of the physical and sexual traumas that go along with a child being abused are present here too. I've been saying this for about three years. Now I really know that I'm right.

It's a basic skill to survive, a basic right. If the essence of life is to maximize your potential, you cannot do so without basic literacy skills, socially, intellectually, every other way.

I didn't wind up in prison like [some of] my fellow illiterates, but I feel the pain of being locked up in a sense—certainly intellectually.

While I am by other people's standards "successful," I had a false passport. Despite my accomplishments, an inferiority complex has kept me down.

I went through the system and cheated in how I learned. I didn't sort this out until the last 3 years. The emotional part I'm feeling is like I stole first base, which is outside the rules; I stole second base, which is within the rules; I stole third base and that's where I am now. I must come home, and that's what literacy means to me.

America, the literate society, that is, has really underestimated the problem. They know intellectually but don't know emotionally what it means to be illiterate.

It means access to the greatest natural resource in this country, the brain—your own brain and the brains of others—were denied to me. I have a lot of excitement about what's going on in the country now.

Literacy is a grassroots movement. It's appropriate that the libraries are a leading player. If we're going to break the cycle of failure in our society, we have to send the messages to a lot of places.

Eventually we are going to have to prevent illiteracy. I've been trying to talk to educators, and they've said to me, "This adult learning, John, it's just not going to happen, it's not going to do it."

And I've said, "Well, it did it for me."

Education has to come into it at some point. The whole thing ought to raise some questions like how do people learn to read? How do people learn? When I see a circle I see 360 degrees. For me 15 of these degrees are blurred.

We do intellectually acknowledge the fact that people

are all different, that our brains are different, but I was taught in a system that didn't allow for my difference.

My story illustrates that there is no one answer because I learned another way.

I've turned from an activist and a spokesperson to a missionary for the cause. It's time for us to become more organized. I've talked to new readers across the country. I think we could use a speakers bureau in our process.

Also more formal training, less by the seat of the pants. I met over 100 new readers at an event in Washington, D.C., all of whom would make excellent spokespersons.

After the process of emotional healing, I believe we could make a contribution. We new readers can offer solutions to the problems we've all participated in.

We need to formulate some ideas along these lines. Not that there's anything to apologize for. We've done real good.

We are always dyslexic. By the way, we never get over it, we just learned to cope and to figure out things. I have a lot of dyslexia symptoms—auditory discrimination problems, and many more on the checklist. Part of my dyslexia problem is that I can't remember what's on the checklist.

I was a real problem for my 2nd, 3rd, and 4th grade teachers. So I was a problem in school.

I had to be on guard all of the time.

Eventually every segment of the society will have to participate in this literacy movement. I've hired a marketing consultant to do a study to find out where I can be most effective and useful.

I have some administrative and entrepreneurial background. And I've given myself permission to bring my other business skills that I've developed over my lifetime toward this holy land I call literacy. I've done over 100 talks now, and I've given myself permission to make literacy my business.

If I'm telling people literacy is good business, then I'd better make it my business, all of my business.

What I've traditionally done in my own business is hire consultants to do studies, from engineers to sales and marketing people. Now I'm learning how to write and put creative things on a piece of paper.

I'm still not spelling well.

About spelling—You literate community are wrong when you assume the attitude that spelling is less important than reading or creative writing. You give permission for illiteracy thereby. It's like stopping at a certain place. In other cases, attitudes of teachers give permission not to learn to read.

The definition of literacy is reading and writing and spelling, it's communicating your thoughts and your ideas. It also enhances your oral communication skills. In thinking, if you talk to yourself in small terms, you're thinking small. If you have a limited vocabulary, you are going to have limited conversations with yourself.

I'm big on basic skills. There's no glamour in it, but my feeling is, teach him basic skills, and self-esteem will come along. It's the foundation. Lots of people would rather start with the roof.

For my future business I'd like to join a scientist who could help sort out some of this stuff (a hard scientist, not an educator or social scientist) and plot and document the role of basic skills in self-esteem.

I'd like to summarize the mechanics of learning how to read.[51] I have a friend who's a pediatric neurologist who believes that everyone can learn how to read if taught properly.[52]

I'd like to share with you some of the projects I have in progress right now. There's a 12-step project which deals with healing for adults.

We're going to develop a training film for volunteers, working with the Director of Los Angeles Rehabilitation Center-Public Health. He's now connected alcohol and drugs to literacy. It began by his noticing that 80% of his alcohol and drug clients couldn't read the "Big Book."

Probably the nicest thing you can say about an illiterate person in America is that he's underemployed. Others are on drugs, in jail, etc.

Whenever I'm asked "Why did it take you so long to learn how to read?" I answer, "Why did it take literate America so long to invite me?"

We are fragile. We need to be protected and encouraged.

We didn't have that in school. By the 3rd and 4th grades, it was all over for us. We were "dumb" or "lazy."

People wonder why we hide. We got the shame, and we carry the blame.

We need to know when the literate world is telling the truth, or not. Some of the success of the volunteer tutors is that they don't carry the "educational" baggage. The only cure for illiteracy is literacy.

I have forgiven the literate world for any real or imagined trespasses they made against me. Now it's time for them to forgive me.

When I speak to educators, they are afraid that I'm going to blame them. I'm not going to.

Teachers are fragile too.

I thought before that the literate world was my enemy. I used to think there was a conspiracy not to teach people to read. I don't feel that way any more. Now I know that illiteracy is the enemy. It is our rage. We illiterates got dealt an unfair hand.

When I talk to people in prisons, they know the rage too, but they acted it out. I think with literacy we're going to solve more problems than we ever imagined.

New readers want to participate in society.

Now I write letters and it takes me 10 or 12 hours for each one. I can get a secretary to do this for me, and sometimes I do, but I also try. It's important.

What literacy has done for me is make me feel a member of society now. And that's why I want to participate.

A Native Alien

Native Alien here from there
You can be found everywhere,
Going through the motions,
Showing your emotions.

Oh! Native Alien, you are lame,
And literate Society plays its games.
They still keep looking for someone to blame,
Isn't that the shame?
Don't they have any idea of our pain?
It seems so plain,
But they keep looking for someone to blame,
What a national shame.

They give us our promotions,
And put us through the motions.
Bluebirds here, Redbirds there,
And now we have Jail Birds everywhere.

Oh! How we tried.
Oh! How we cried.
We were just past five,
And how we had to hide.
Oh! And how we had to hide.
Oh! How they stole our pride.
Oh! How they lied.

Native Alien, here from there,
Native Alien everywhere.
Shame, shame, we can't read,
And how this nation bleeds.
But they still will not heed,
Why Johnny, the Native Alien,
Still can't read.

Oh! How he tried.
Oh! How many times he died.
Literate society, you can't hide.
Oh! Literate society, how come you lie?
Scapegoat, cover up, alibi, too.
Oh! Literate society, shame on you.
Oh! Literate society, you can't hide
Illiteracy statistics, have your hide,
While you choke on your own pride.

Native Alien, he can't read.
It limits him, we concede,
But he has ideas, concepts and theories, too!
And that's the stuff of thought
That you ought to concede to.

I wrote this in 1987. It was the first thing I wrote. I don't feel this angry anymore with the literate world. Once I learned to read I got rid of most of these feelings.

Now I'm dealing with the rest and getting rid of them too. I'm beginning to sort things out. I'm interested in facilitating now. I think we're living in an extraordinary time. I think that there's a window of opportunity open for the literate society to improve our education system.

Afterword

With the growth of the population in California over 650,000 persons per year, the state now represents over ten percent of the population of United States. Immigration from abroad and from other states bring a growing diversity of people needing a broad range of services. Those needing literacy services represent all facets of the challenge. Libraries, along with other literacy providers in California have created a diverse system in response to the enormity of the demand.

The notes are included to amplify upon the text and in no way are meant to detract from the messages brought directly from the new readers.

Notes

1. Elena Tsherny, acquisitions librarian for the Washington, D.C. Public Library, conducts market research about non-English-speaking reader and ESL students' needs by attending church services in ethnic neighborhoods, sitting for hours talking to walk-in patients in neighborhood clinics, and otherwise finding ways of getting to her constituents on their own ground.

2. Numerous studies, reports, and articles have appeared documenting the number and description of illiteracy in America. It is not the purpose of this book to detail this information or to question whether there is a problem.

3. Kentucky is an example where a court decision has just declared all state education laws unconstituional and ordered the state education department to cease to exist on June 30.

4. Commissioned by the Secretary who was under pressure to prove that the nation's educational system was inadequate. This report stunned everyone by stating, "Our Nation is at risk. Our once unchallenged preeminence in commerce, industry, science, and technological innovation is being overtaken by competitors throughout the world." Further, the report stated, "... individuals in our society who do not possess the levels of skill, literacy, and training essential to this new era will be effectively disenfranchised, ... from the chance to participate fully in our national life."

5. The Orton Dyslexia Society is involved with educating Americans and has, through its advocacy efforts has helped change this experience for thousands of parents and children. The American Association for Children With Learning Disabilities has an educational program which is designed to sensitize the public. In 1991 the David Jacobs/Lorimar Studios production of "Guns of Paradise" on CBS has an evolving story-line of George, a nine-year old boy facing the embarrassment of dyslexia in an 1890s context. His brothers and sisters help him hide and respond effectively to his experience. Early labels on children have significant on-going impact on the futures of children and how they are viewed in the world.

6. Many learners come into the literacy programs with the expressed desire to improve their spelling. Often an inability to spell is associated with a lack of reading experience—little opportunity to see the words one needs to spell repeatedly in print. Sometimes the learner has no understanding of basic phonics rules and can not apply these to help with spelling. Most often, lack of spelling ability is a combination of these and other factors.

7. Writing and reading development go hand in hand. Most literacy programs recognize this and teach the basic skills of both concurrently. The whole language approach employs the learner's own experiences which are written down in exercises called "language experience." At first these will be written down by the tutor. The learner and tutor practice reading the passage together and then the learner reads it alone. Once the learner writes the passage himself, the tutor explains spelling, punctuation, and grammar rules as they apply to that passage. Many library programs have adopted this very successful approach because learners like working with material which is innately interesting to them—their own words/experiences.

8. The best support employers can provide is to recognize the reliable, hard-working employee who has temporary reading, writing, and computational skills defects. The informed employer knows that (according to the American Society for Training and Development) it takes three times more money to recruit, select, and hire a new employee as it will to retrain the current worker who is already familiar with the context of his work.

   Even more striking is the realization that 7 out of 10 workers employed today will still be working in 2010 according to the

Workforce 2000 report of the Hudson Institute. So even if schools, kindergarten through grade 12, were the best they could be tomorrow, there remains the challenge of dealing with the workforce now in place.

9. The National Assessment of Educational Progress (NAEP study) found that youngsters whose parents are functionally illiterate are twice as likely as their peers to be functionally illiterate. The importance of family in the early preliteracy development of children has been noted by many researchers into adult literacy. Parents are the child's first teachers and the love of books and reading is clearly established in most avid readers long before they ever see a school classroom. Children who enter school without having experienced books and printed words take many years to "catch up" in basic readiness skills. Often, by the time they are ready to learn to read, the class has gone off and left them, and they get further and further behind. Most of the adults in this book cite their recognition at an early grade level of being "behind" the others in reading. Most were aware of their difference by the fourth or fifth grade.

10. The California Senate Select Committee on Small Business and the Joint Economic Committee on California's Future is what is meant.

11. The California Senate Task Force on Workforce Literacy. Probably for the first time in the nation an adult learner who was succeeding at work was asked to present his view to a policy making body. Until this time, expert testimony had not included the person being testified about. Involvement of adult learners in policy and programming has been a primary focus of the California Literacy Campaign and Laubach Literacy Action and is also a key element of Literacy Volunteers of America, Lutheran Church Women's Literacy Programs, as well as many others.

12. The employer also reaps rewards from the employee's performance at work.

13. More and more new readers are discovering the joys of knowledge and independence that accompany learning to read. They are entering into leadership roles to seek solutions and are accepting challenges and rising above the fear and confusion of illiteracy. They are being heard.

14. In September 1990, radio station KBIG-Los Angeles and KOIT-San Francisco, who are identified as the most listened to stations at work in California, carried on a consistent and reliable series of messages that highlight the stories of adults who are succeeding at work and that it is the employers who also benefit over the long haul. In Los Angeles 60% of all learner calls during that month to a literacy hot-line phone indicated they had heard the KBIG message.

    In 1987 the National Association of Broadcasters Productivity In The Workplace Initiative found that showing people succeeding at retraining efforts resulted in the best response in a five-city study.

    California Literacy Campaign has contributed significantly toward the development and implementation of cross-media campaigns in many parts of California. Partners have included ABC, NBC, and CBS local affiliates, newspapers, radio stations, members of the California Grocer's Association.

    Unions, particularly members of the AFL-CIO have undertaken joint ventures with companies.

15. More often than not, an employee who lacks basic literacy skills hides that fact for fear of being discovered and embarrassed. Improving her/his skills enhances the ability to work well. Helping people think smarter creates a "win" situation for everyone.

16. In most communities library literacy programs work very closely with local adult education schools and community colleges to see that adults get the type of support and training which best fits their needs. Libraries make referrals everyday to these and other types of support/self-help programs from which an adult learner can benefit. In addition, tutors often continue to support the learner after "graduation" from a literacy program when they enter another school or program.

17. Many quality children's materials are available for the adult learner to read to her/his children. An accessible source of these materials is the public library.

    Even a non-reader can start by sharing a wordless picture book such as *The Snowman* with a child. Another book, *More, More, More*, a Caldecott honor book for 1990, is an example of a beautifully illustrated and well-written book which an adult with only a first grade reading ability can easily learn to read to his children.

Given the needs and abilities of the adult, a children's librarian can be a wonderful resource person in the selection of quality, but simple, books for reading aloud to children.

18. The experience of many adult literacy programs around the nation is that for many children who enter school eager to learn, the classroom becomes the place where their enthusiasm and desires are stifled rather than enhanced. To complete the cycle, teachers who are overburdened, underpaid, and under-appreciated often have a difficult time establishing a positive, firm learning atmosphere in their classrooms.

    A 1983 issue of *Time* pointed out that "nationwide, education majors come from the lowest strata of college students, scoring 32 points below national average on the verbal portion of the SAT, and 48 points lower on the math section." (Michigan Literacy, Inc.)

19. Adults often acquire or enhance other cognitive abilities such as listening, short and long term critical thinking and memory even as they struggle with reading and writing skills deficiencies.

    The challenge is to consider the strength of what they bring to the task and how these abilities can help get the job done—Part of thinking smarter.

    Working to learn.
    Learning to work.
    The smarter paradigm.

20. Experience shows that when adults decide to learn to read better it is a courageous decision filled with the best motivation yet they still carry the hurt and shame of illiteracy with them. Thus it is critical that all staff, regardless of the agency, be welcoming and supportive from the simplest exchange onward. Excellent customer relations and service will be the best advertisement for a program.

21. Many new adult readers testify to the effectiveness of one-on-one tutoring. But the right match is critical to the success of a one-on-one tutoring experience. Most often a learner initiates the process by calling or showing up at a library asking for help. An initial assessment determines if the learner has basic English literacy needs or should be referred to a more advanced program at an adult school or community college. Once the learner is assessed, the literacy program staff tries to find a trained volunteer tutor who can meet at times and places convenient to that learner.

The idea is to reduce the barriers to attending the sessions as much as possible, as the adult learner has enough barriers to overcome already without adding new ones!

Sometimes an immediate match is found and the tutor calls the learner and begins right away. Sometimes it may take many weeks or occasionally even months to find a good match. Other factors such as personal likes and dislikes, hobbies and interests are also considered in making the match. In addition, the learner is told that if he/she is not comfortable with a tutor or cannot work well with this person, all he/she has to do is call the program back and request a different tutor.

22. Computer Assisted Instruction (CAI) has become a vital part of many literacy programs. Adults like it because it is non-threatening and non-judgmental. They also like the fact that they are learning basic skills at the same time they are becoming computer literate. Many jobs in our nation today require a level of computer literacy and these adult learners feel good about saying they have that. It is also a source of pride for their children to say their mommy or daddy works with a computer.

23. Ginger once again points out the vital role the parent plays in the development of the child. Many adult learners enter literacy programs with the expressed purpose of reading to their children or helping them with their homework. Their children are very often the motivating factor that finally pushes the adult illiterate or semi-literate to make that first, difficult step toward receiving literacy help.

24. A vital part of any literacy program is the assessment component. Adults cannot be easily categorized into a grade level as it is applied to school children but usually have a variety of skills and each may be at a different level. Lloyd, for instance might have no knowledge of basic phonics (level 0) but could have a sight vocabulary of about fourth level and comprehension ability at an even higher level on materials with which he was familiar. For this reason assessment of present skills, interests, and needs of the adult learner plays a major role in his/her tutoring program. Recently developed literacy workplace programs, such as Workplace Resources of Simon and Schuster, have designed new tests to measure adult literacy needs based on life experience.

25. The true objective of learning to read is to acquire that tool which will enable one to become a self-learner. The goal is not found in the skills themselves but in helping the adult acquire those tools necessary to become independent. It is wonderful when an adult learner comes to treasure the joy of reading for pleasure, but more often then not their goals are much more practical and related to specific life or job needs.

26. Trusted, credible word of mouth referral is the best recruiter that we have for literacy program enrollment.

27. One key element of any successful literacy program is an abundance of positive reinforcement. Tutors must be carefully trained in the importance of being a cheerleader for their learner. So often the greatest hindrance to reading or writing is the adult's lack of self-confidence. In the most effective programs, tutors are taught to recognize this and to spend much time and energy demonstrating to the learner what she/he does know and can do building on this.

28. One very important role of any literacy provider is to work in conjunction with other social service agencies. Adults seeking services from one agency often need the services of other agencies as well. It is not very efficient or effective to have one agency trying to meet all of the needs of an individual, but through careful cross-training of staff and understanding of the programs offered by various agencies, prompt and appropriate referrals can be quickly and easily made.

29. Counselors, doctors, and nurses can make excellent referrals based on their knowledge and observation of patient activity. However, it is equally apparent that the same people lack the means to identify people with literacy difficulties. Helping professionals realize the benefits to them in identifying and referring clients is often seen in better functioning and decision-making of these clients. Also professionals need to know where people can call for help so toll-free access to referral is vital to a successful program.

30. All too often adults express the feeling of being all alone with their problem and that no one else has it. These adults are relieved when they meet other adults trying to improve their reading skills.

31. Statistics indicate that over 60% of all incarcerated adults are illiterate or semi-literate and 85% of all juvenile offenders have reading problems. (U.S. Department of Education) Bob was offered help in the institutions, but he saw no reason to take advantage of it. There was no peer pressure to learn to read—actually there was pressure not to be involved in school at all.

32. Today there are other things being taught in institutions besides just the "tricks of the trade." Many local, state and federal institutions offer educational opportunities for non readers from GED programs to college-level classes.

In Contra Costa County where Bob lives, the present adult facilities offer a wide variety of classes and the inmate who participates is given "good time" (or time off his sentence) for attending these. The local library program, Project Second Chance, in which Bob was eventually tutored, works closely with the Contra Costa County Office of Education to provide both one-on-one tutoring by outside volunteers as well as an excellent peer tutoring program where inmates are trained as volunteer tutors and then tutor other inmates. Both receive "good time" for their efforts. However, what is often most noted is the tremendous increase in self-confidence in the both the inmate tutor and the inmate learner. Many public library programs participate in some way in providing literacy services to jails and prisons.

33. The Governor's National Educational Summit with President Bush identified literacy as one of five goals for change over the next ten years.

34. Bob's efforts with his own employer, the newspaper company Lesher Communications, Inc. (LCI), have resulted in that company's support of many literacy programs: LCI developed and published effective recruitment ads; was instrumental in establishing and funding the start-up of a county-wide network; published a year-long series of feature articles which looked at all aspects of literacy; and since 1987 has featured a weekly column called "The Informed Reader." This column, like that of the *Philadelphia Inquirer* presents a topic of current interest directed at a fourth to sixth grade readability level. They have proved popular with teachers and school-age children as well as adults.

35. This incident was just one example of the importance of the appropriate tutor/learner match. Bob was matched with an experienced tutor but somehow they did not get along. Both tutor and learner realized this so when Bob called the literacy office to request a different tutor, no time was wasted in finding a different match. Bob's second tutor, Diane, was just perfect. They became very good friends in a short time and still stay in touch three years later.

36. The importance and impact of the social exchanges can never be underestimated. They can only be enlivened.

37. One of the best sources of recruitment for adult literacy programs is word of mouth. A trusted and reliable friend or acquaintance is the most often identified source of linkage to literacy programs. As learners like Darlene find success and a feeling of accomplishment in their tutoring sessions, they talk to others who might also need the help. Initially, many are concerned about acknowledging their illiteracy in public, but then with the support of family and employers often become speakers at conferences, leaders of workshops, and general spokespersons for the adult literacy movement.

    Library literacy programs employ many recruitment strategies, but the personal message from one adult to another is still one of the most successful. The media has also become instrumental in learner recruitment nationally. When learners who used to be afraid to admit "I cannot read" begin to acknowledge that although nothing to be proud of, it is an accepted part of them, they become advocates to a wider audience.

    Television shows and movies which sensitively portray illiteracy have helped make this possible. As a result, more adults come to realize that their problems are not necessarily their own fault and that it is okay to seek help. Newspapers and radio continue expanding efforts to make the issue highly visible.

38. Hopefully, "this kind of thing" no longer happens to adults when they approach a literacy program. A better understanding of the nature of the adult illiterate or semi-literate as well as better training of staff and volunteers in how to be sensitive to their needs has made this sort of embarrassing situation an exception rather than the norm.

39. Literacy advancement disrupts personal, social, and community relationships. As dependency on others to read for you and do for you evaporates, the nature of the bonds between people are upset. Sometimes the reader's significant others may not want the dependent person to become independent and prefers the old days and old ways now gone—so this person fights for the status quo and obstacles for success are put in the way—demands on time, attention (e.g. baby sitting) appear.

40. Many Army enlistees can't read training manuals written at the seventh grade level. (*New York Times* June 10, 1980. Section A p.19.)

41. Drinking/Driving Program (DDP), run by OSHA, is a program of counseling and group therapy with a minimal amount of private therapy.

42. A for-pay tutoring program in California that offers small group instruction for children having difficulty in school.

43. Giving back in an unassuming and generous way, the community wins as well.

44. Thirteen percent of all 17-year olds are functionally illiterate. Among minority youth, the figure may run as high as 40%. (National Commission on Excellence in Education)

45. Often times adults believe they can read even when they have significant problems. The key to motivation is to help these adults realize that they can improve their reading ability. In the confidential and private exchanges with program people, the real difficulties get to be shared and acted upon with individual learning and goal-centered tutoring or group instruction.

46. It is not unusual for adults who enroll in AA or another recovery group to also seek literacy help. Most of these programs depend on an individual's ability to read the related literature that the program provides. When an adult is clearly unable to handle the reading requirements, he/she is often referred to a literacy program where a tutor can be assigned to help her/him deal with the print requirements as well as improving the person's reading in general. Someone who is truly ready to take the step to recovery through AA is often ready to make other changes in his/her life.

Many clients exhibit reading avoidance behavior in group therapy like forgetting their glasses, going to the bathroom, being disruptive when faced with reading.

47. As the population in homeless shelters has risen, so has the awareness that many homeless people are less than literate and that this can be a big factor in their seeking employment and/or job training. Jonathan Kozol pointed out that 75% of unemployed adults have reading or writing difficulties. (*Illiterate America)* The federal government has sought to remedy this in a number of ways, including the passage of the McKinney Act which grants money through the states to qualified shelters to provide literacy services. In addition, some libraries and adult schools have brought literacy and tutoring for adults into the shelters. Some libraries and other community organizations take children's programming such as storytimes and lapsits to the shelters to aid in the pre-literacy development of homeless children.

48. Many children in homeless shelters have never lived anywhere but in a shelter all of their five, eight, and even ten years of life. They have never known any other home nor any other kind of family life. It is hard for them to go to regular schools because they don't have the proper clothes and change addresses often. Many stay in one shelter a few weeks and then move on to another shelter somewhere else. Often they do not go to school at all. Jonathan Kozol's *Rachel and Her Children* deals with this issue most effectively.

49. Although English as a Second Language (ESL) is an increasing need in this country especially in states such as California, the fact remains that the majority of illiterates continue to be English-speaking. According to a U.S. Census Bureau survey, 13% of all American adults are illiterate. The rate for Spanish-speaking adults who first language is not English is 54%. For other adults whose native tongue is not English, the rate is 41%.

50. Economic suffering, making better consumer buying choices and health care decisions are elements of the modalities to learn and grow. The community benefits in many ways—new dollars for taxes, better skilled employees and the practicing of health care prevention activity rather than emergency care.

51. William Wilson of WKET-TV, Kentucky Educational Television, is an educator who lectures widely on developments in learning. At the 1991 AAACE (American Association of Adult and Continuing Education) Conference in Hartford, Connecticut, he presented figures showing that 70% of learning comes from visual symbols.

52. There is much to support the notion that almost anyone can learn to read if taught properly. However, to be taught properly an individual must have his/her learning needs and learning strengths assessed and sometimes a very individualized program must be developed. With adults this is one reason why one-on-one tutoring has proven most effective. In very young children the desire to learn is there. In adults it is often there but overshadowed by doubt and prior failures. The adult erects many barriers consciously and unconsciously, and then barriers must be broken down for learning to take place.

Barbara Prete

Gary E. Strong

About the Editors

Barbara Prete became interested in literacy when she was Director of the National Book Awards from 1983-89. In discovering that writing is a struggle and a challenge even for the nation's most distinguished authors, she began developing programs that would enable prize-winning writers to share their experiences with learners, both children and adults. Toward this end, she helped found, and served as first director of, the National Book Foundation and National Book Week.

Ms. Prete writes a regular column on literacy for *Publisher's Weekly* magazine and contributes articles on the subject to *Library Journal* and others. She is interviewed widely in the media about new literate Americans.

Gary E. Strong is State Librarian of California. Under his leadership, the public libraries of California have created the California Literacy Campaign. Funded with state appropriations under the California Library Services Act, over eighty public libraries assist adult learners take bold new steps in improving their reading and writing ability and assisting them in moving into the broader avenues of learning. The Campaign is built around adults achieving their own goals toward learning while encouraging a lifetime of reading and writing. Believing that libraries could take a more active role, Strong and his colleagues worked for the successful passage of the California Library Literacy Service Act and the Families for Literacy Act, both of which have been cited as pioneering examples for the nation. A frequent lecturer and writer, Strong uses every opportunity to bring public and private resources together on behalf of literacy.